CLEAN COLORED GIRL CHRONICLES?

The Clean Colored Girl Chronicles are stories from one woman's life as she shares how relationships made her and broke her. As she learned how to navigate through being a daughter with parent issues, a black woman, single woman, dating woman, married yet unhappy woman, divorced woman and an entrepreneur, she is a clean colored girl, making it in the world. Trials keep you strong when you learn to endure them, and that she does.

Clean Colored Girl

Being a Clean Colored Girl is being courageous, perseverant and remaining openhearted, even when it hurts, facing interesting and difficult situations in life and becoming resilient as a result.

Broken Conditions

Broken Conditions are often rooted in family dynamics and many times we don't know the effects of the past until life happens and it's difficult to cope or heal. People don't mind breaking others because they are already broken and we all know, misery loves company. Once broken, restoration is possible – by putting the past where it belongs, because it has passed. Peeling through the pain is what most people need to do in order to get beyond their Broken Conditions.

Why is resilience important?

Resilience is the ability to become strong, healthy, or successful again after something bad happens. You matter. Overcoming life's challenges takes resilience.

PRAISE FOR JO LENA JOHNSON'S BROKEN CONDITIONS

"*Broken Conditions* is an honest account of the life experiences of a "clean colored girl." The author doesn't try to reinvent the wheel here. She simply tells the stories that many women, colored or otherwise, can relate to. The stories that shape who we become over and over again; growing up a product of divorce, the struggle of the mother-daughter relationship, and MEN! These are stories of failure and brokenness and growth and resilience. Johnson's storytelling is such that you'll place yourself in the back seat of that Cadillac with the trumpet player's friend as he starts to urinate in a cup. You'll experience the terror of hiding in the bathroom as a drug-addicted man kicks in the back door. You can taste the excitement of living out your dreams in Los Angeles and the fulfillment of finding God and purpose. This is a good and quick read that will leave you wanting Volume 2."

- ***Faith Conner, Host, The Platform 314 Podcast***

"Reading *Broken Conditions* is like having a good, long talk with a close girlfriend, sharing secrets while sworn to secrecy. The stories are intensely personal—some biting, some tender. Though the author's experiences are unique, they're also the universal tales of wisdom every soulful woman will find encouraging and inspiring."

- ***Mara Purl, Best-selling, Award-winning Author of the Milford-Haven Novels***

"The level of honesty in this book might surprise you: truthfulness about mistakes, family challenges, rush to judgment, less-than-perfect relationships. But Jo Lena Johnson shares her life— the good, bad and ugly —with an unwavering frankness that we can all learn from. Not only will you see the author in *Broken Conditions*, but you will also see yourself. This is recommended reading, and I am eagerly awaiting *The Lady and the Chief,* the second volume of *The Clean Colored Girl Chronicles*!"

- ***Daryle Glynn Brown, News Producer***

"Broken Conditions is the perfect book for a quick weekend read. Jo Lena does an excellent job of being relatable and real. In fact, I almost felt like she and I were sitting on my couch with a cup of Joe while she told me about her life. From struggles as a child and rocky relationships in her 30s to triumph as a business woman, *Broken Conditions* takes you on a journey that shows you exactly why Jo Lena Johnson is the "Absolute Good Resilience Coach."

- ***Katy Beigel***

"Broken Conditions is fantastic! It reminds me of books like *Eat, Love, Pray* by Elizabeth Gilbert or *Waiting to Exhale* by Terry McMillan. It's real and keeps you reading. How lucky Jo Lena is to have an amazing and interesting life. She was always starting "projects," i.e. relationships, endeavors, etc. in the book that weren't always necessarily for the betterment of her soul. Just her filling the holes. Channeling this book into a movie; now that's a better project. Everyone is soul searching and will connect with her story."

- ***Shannon Tocco***

"I'm sorry, but then again, I'm not sorry, because God has a way of using us and our stories for his good. In reading *Broken Conditions,* I saw myself, my mother, the stepfather and men in my own life. After growing up in a whirlwind, I had to make conscious decisions not just for myself, but for my three sons. I didn't want to succumb to drinking, drugs, and being a whore. The love and respect I had for my kids made me respect me. I have this survivors guilt, *How did I go through so much in life without going crazy, going to jail, or being dead?* My discovery is, I've been kept by God to share the only truth I know. This life doesn't belong to me, and I must share his grace and mercy even when I don't fully understand the purpose or plan of the journey. I love you so much for sharing, and allowing me to be a part of your journey."

- ***Delena Evans***

"Reading *Broken Conditions* made me feel like I wasn't alone, not that I would want someone to ever go through my situation of life, but the reality is that these issues are more prominent than most will admit. The book made me think about the many ladies and gentlemen like me going through obstacles and over hurdles because of the dysfunctional conditions in which we were raised. Adversity affects the way we see ourselves and the way we look at tomorrow. I am inspired. I have the courage to look toward the future and to welcome it, one step at a time."

- ***Robin Thomas***

"I found *Broken Conditions* riveting. I hung on the author's every word which was rooted in candor and vulnerability. Jo Lena Johnson courageously shares her story with humor and truth. She inspires each of us to assess the root cause of our own broken conditions and to then, courageously, do something about it. I cannot wait for her next book!"

- Nadine Roberts Cornish,
Author of Tears In My Gumbo

"Frank and honest, *Broken Conditions* chronicles the relationships, loves, and struggles of its resilient author, Jo Lena Johnson. Jo Lena makes you feel like an intimate friend as she regales you with stories of growing up a product of divorce, her relationship failures and her career successes. The biggest reason I had trouble relating to the book is not because I'm white but because I've been married to my second-ever boyfriend since I was 21 years old, so although I've had plenty of struggles, I have little dating experience. But, like most women, I can relate to how past relationships affect future ones. And I found Jo Lena's can-do attitude when tackling a new career or project, no matter how risky, to be inspiring."

- Karen L. Tucker, Comma Queen

The Mission is Possible.

Sharing love and wisdom for the young and "the young at heart," expanding minds, restoring kindness through good thoughts, feelings, and attitudes is our intent. May you thrive and be good in all you are and all you do…

Be Cause U.R. Absolute Good!

The Clean Colored Girl Chronicles, Volume 1: Broken Conditions
© 2018 by Jo Lena Johnson

No part of this book may be reproduced in any written, electronic, recording, or photocopying form without written permission of the publisher. The exception would be in the case of brief quotations embodied in critical articles or reviews and pages where permission is specifically granted by the publisher.

Although every precaution has been taken to verify the accuracy of the information contained herein, the author and publisher assume no responsibility for any errors or omissions. No liability is assumed for damages that may result from the use of information contained within.

Scripture taken from the Holy Bible, NEW INTERNATIONAL VERSION®, NIV® Copyright © 1973, 1978, 1984, 2011 by Biblica, Inc.® and EASY-TO-READ VERSION™, ERV™ Copyright © 2006 by Bible League International. Used by permission. All rights reserved worldwide.

Books may be purchased in quantity by contacting the publisher directly:

Mission Possible Press, A division of Absolute Good,

PO Box 8039 St. Louis, MO 63156

or by calling 240.644.2500

MissionPossiblePress.com

Cover Photo: Jo Lena Johnson circa 1997, age 27 years old, Los Angeles, California.

Website: JoLenaJohnson.com

ISBN: 978-0-9861818-8-7

First Edition   Printed in the United States

Publisher's Cataloging-In-Publication Data

(Prepared by The Donohue Group, Inc.)

Names: Johnson, Jo Lena, 1970-

Title: Broken conditions / Jo Lena Johnson.

Description: First edition. | St. Louis, MO : Mission Possible Press, [2018] | Series: The clean colored girl chronicles ; volume 1

Identifiers: ISBN 9780986181887 (print) | ISBN 9780999676608 (ebook) | ISBN 9780986181894 (audiobook)

Subjects: LCSH: Johnson, Jo Lena, 1970- | African American women college students--Biography. | Resilience (Personality trait) | Emotional maturity. | Interpersonal relations. | LCGFT: Autobiographies.

Classification: LCC E185.97 .J64 2018 (print) | LCC E185.97 (ebook) | DDC 305.896073/0092--dc23

Broken CONDITIONS

THE CLEAN COLORED GIRL CHRONICLES
VOLUME 1

Broken CONDITIONS

JO LENA JOHNSON

MISSION POSSIBLE PRESS

Creating Legacies through Absolute Good Works

Dedication

To every creative genius who has struggled to find your way, you have so much to offer. Don't allow the lines to keep you boxed in, and don't allow your talents to isolate you. It's time for you to Rise Up!

Contents

Dear Reader 1

Truth in Love 4

Broken Conditions 7

Speak Up 12

Heart and Mind Dis-Ease 15

The Trumpet Player 25

Family Dynamics 42

He Wasn't My Husband 46

Looking for Love 57

Dark Spaces 75

Peeling Through the Pain 93

Epilogue 97

Excerpt from Volume 2: *Lady and the Chief* 103

Discussion/Book Club Questions 108

About the Author 111

"Love never gives up on people. It never stops trusting, never loses hope, and never quits." – 1 Cor. 13:7 (ERV)

Dear Reader

Being a Clean Colored Girl is being courageous, perseverant and remaining openhearted, even when it hurts, facing interesting and difficult situations in life and becoming resilient as a result.

When something juicy, unexpected or surprising happens in my life and I'm speaking to one of my close friends, I start telling the story by saying, *"I was minding my own clean colored business when..."* because I'm a clean colored girl working to make my way in this world, and because I like saying it. I'm a genuine person who is direct and outspoken because I care. Being that way has caused me problems. And I've made thousands of mistakes, requiring acknowledgment, adjustment and apology at times. Being courageous, perseverant and remaining openhearted, *even when it hurts*, is largely because of my belief in God's promises and demonstrations.

My name is Jo Lena Johnson. My first name is Jo and my middle name is Lena. I was born in Des Moines, Iowa, and grew up in St. Louis, Missouri. I was a Girl Scout, a huge cookie seller, and I opened and entered every Publisher's Clearing House Sweepstakes to grace our mailbox in the '80s. I was placed in Honors classes in 7th grade and was kicked out of each one for talking back to the teachers except English, where I had my first Black female teacher. Turning around my act in high school, I was one of the most active students on campus, becoming Junior Class President, Student Council Fundraising Chairperson, Yearbook Photography Editor and Pep Club President, my favorite role ever.

I graduated from the University of Missouri-Columbia. After college, I moved to Los Angeles, California, where I met the stars, hung around in bars and found the Lord. Marketing was my primary focus back then, and I worked in the engineering, beverage and radio industries while finding my way in the City of Angels. I have been running my own business during nearly 20 years of highs, lows, ups, downs and quite a few woes. I've conducted training sessions and workshops in 47 states, four provinces in Canada and 17 cities in the United Kingdom, directly touching nearly 100,000 people, sharing how to communicate effectively, manage conflict and maintain even after something bad happens (resilience). I love to be in love and to be loved in return. I've been married and divorced twice. I've never been pregnant, and I don't have any children. My steadiest Friday night date is my little niece with whom I enjoy great adventures, usually leading to McDonald's before the evening is over—though she'll take Applebee's, because she loves those table games, or Chick-fil-A, where she likes to jump around in the kids' play area. I'm a Leo, my favorite color is red, and I'm a sorority girl. Thank you for sharing your life and time with me.

Blessings,

Jo Lena Johnson

Truth in Love

"Self-reflection is one of the most important habits one can develop… May your heart be touched and your soul be enlightened by the joys, sorrows and victories, as becoming resilient takes hard work and perseverance."

Have you looked in the mirror and shaken your head … not just at your appearance, but also at what you don't see? I have. Often I have seen the pain, misery and confusion that has cloaked me because of my own choices. At times, I have been sick to my stomach—vomiting sick—realizing that I had compromised the best parts of me—all for "love." That's no way to live.

Yet I have often wondered how someone who claims to love me can look me in my face and lie … well, I know how! I do it to myself all the time! What about you?

I have looked at the dark circles, the swollen belly and the turmoil that rises up during the slightest inconvenience, which proved to me that I was not living right. Yet I was helpless and powerless to change my position or circumstance.

There were so many times my voice of reason, discernment and spirit said, "Stop, stand and walk away." Yet I could not and did not. It was because I was relying on my own willpower and limitations.

My mind had been made up, and I was relentless.

I have holes and I have made choices to fill those holes—even when I knew those were temporary or short-term fixes. I'm just grateful that I don't have a predilection for certain things; otherwise, I might have become a drunken, drugged-up, sexed-up, super fat whore of a mother who would cuss you and call myself loving you at the same time.

I had no idea what I deserved because I was focused on my desires. If I got everything and everyone I desired, I would be dead or in jail because somebody would have killed me or I would have killed them. Yes, there is a physical side of madness and also an emotional one. The soul wants what it wants.

This is a narrative, not a one-size-fits-all advice book. These are my stories of life, love, grace and resilience. By reading my chronicles, maybe you can get some perspective to help you with your own—or at least avoid some of my failings and shortcomings. I have some deep thoughts and feelings

I'm willing to share in hopes that if you see/recognize yourself or even get repelled by my states of madness, you may make different or better choices for yourself. My aim is to share with you things I did and failed to do. Why? Because this way, I can leave room for you to make your own judgments. Get uncomfortable! There are two other books in this series, and if you stick with them, you'll likely be uncomfortable on some level. I challenge you to get so mad and disgusted that you begin to feel the pain of what has been ignored if that's what it takes, to peel through the pain. I did it and so can you. Get through this first book because recognizing *Broken Conditions* is critical to getting to the core of who you were born to be. On my website, you'll find ideas, advice and videos offering things you can do to become resilient—developing the ability to become strong, healthy or successful again after something bad happens.

You deserve it.

Broken Conditions

"Once broken, restoration is possible. I am excited to put the past where it belongs, because it has passed. But in between, a whole lot of holes happened."

My programming as a child affected the way I learned to operate and get along with others. I was the only child for seven years and then became the oldest. Things happened, and I learned to try to please people and hope they liked me. I also believed in loyalty—they are just "my people," so no matter what, I'm responsible and they'll always need me. I learned to be resilient, at least by public standards, while breaking on the inside. Not right or wrong, just true for me. The way I processed things, no matter how "they" treated me, it was the best they knew how to do, so I learned to take it, accepting them for who and how they were.

At the age of 32, I enrolled in an intensive four-month leadership program, led by a caring group of folks who do "the work"—the "work of transformation," that is. It helped, as my patterns became better in certain areas because I learned to create boundaries. However, four months didn't erase over 30 years of programming.

Finances, accumulating them and managing them, have been challenging for me and have affected so many aspects of my life. I learned to "give down to the bone," not truly understanding what my wise sibling would say: "Jo, just take care of you." I was the person on the plane giving away the oxygen, underselling my time and talents because "they" needed me. That was what I perceived and how I operated, but it wasn't serving me; I had been suffocating myself.

Self-Care

Giving everything away results in emptiness. Claiming your oxygen is the only way to survive in life-threatening emergencies and in day-to-day living. Filling up with oxygen, purpose and productivity balanced with rest, self-respect, healthy habits and new choices is the way to flow and to grow.

When I began practicing self-care consistently and thought I could make it, new circumstances derailed my progress. More pain in life and poor choices. I told myself I would rise. And I did, for a time. That lasted for a while, but my challenges were far from over. Proudly, I purchased my piece of real estate. I felt accomplished. Being an entrepreneur, I had clients come and go. Some chose not to pay for services even though they received them. However, I didn't have a credit department or henchmen to go and get my money. Today, they can't look me in the face. That behavior is likely based on their own *Broken Conditions*.

Life Happens

Turning 40 brought expectancy, excitement and new experiences. Some were outstanding, while others were difficult to endure. I filed bankruptcy but was able to keep the property, thank God. Realizing the real estate crash played a big role in my circumstances, I got over my shame, searched for alternative streams of income and rebuilt my credit, with help. A friend in the banking industry told me to get a secured credit card and use it to charge existing monthly bills, then pay off the card in full each month, establishing a new pattern of consistency and responsibility. I did so and quickly reestablished my good credit score.

At midlife, I was ready to settle down … again. I chose the wrong man. We didn't make it. I denied, cried, prayed and persevered through the breakup and moved on. I was not going to settle again! Temptations are everywhere, and it's easy to be susceptible. That's covered in *Volume 2*, by the way.

At 45, I married and divorced in the same year. Watch the "who" before you say "I do," that's what I learned … associations, exchanges, invitations and interludes. Many complain that people are "crazy, warped, tired, thirsty," which I've learned often ends up being the case after having associated with those who don't love themselves and have no capacity to love someone else.

People don't mind breaking others because they are already broken, and we all know misery loves company.

Most people grew up with *Broken Conditions* of some kind. Many hold those hurts in and are stunted as a result. I've made 12,594 mistakes … and counting! But I also know how to admit my mistakes, shortcomings, foolish choices and bad decisions—and to lick my wounds.

I've gotten angry, felt rejected and been hurt at the same time! Yet, rejecting bitterness is a necessary action step to live a fulfilling life. I do what I can to heal the holes. Heartache, pain and victories. Not victories because I've "won," but victories because I didn't give up when I wanted to. God has saved me, his daughter, many times and I am grateful. Gratefulness is far more powerful than bitterness.

Breaking Through

What is broken tends to develop into actual conditions. Once that happens, we tend to accept them (*Broken Conditions*) as "just the way things are." However, they don't have to stay that way. If you are willing to be ruthlessly honest with yourself, you can change it.

We can be made or broken by what happens, and we can rise through it with support. For me, that means prayer, faith, friends, wise counsel and perseverance. Letting go when and if the time comes has been challenging, yet we all have our crosses to bear. We can choose to be better than we were last year, yesterday or 10 minutes ago. Creating better habits means implementing new strategies and focusing on the desired outcome, not remaining stuck in outworn conditions. Induce action in thought, feelings, attitude and behavior.

With each seeming defeat, I told myself, *"They can't hold me down. I am ready to rise. I am past the pain and poor choices. I have to rise."* However, there are no "quick fixes" for deeply rooted issues, which become conditions if not yanked out.

I hope you will be inspired by my stories. You will see yourself or someone you know in the books … it's because we are all humans, being! My prayer is for us all to do better—not because we are better, but because we are willing to try!

"If you are willing to be ruthlessly honest with yourself, you can change the effects of Broken Conditions.*"*

Speak Up

"Addressing Broken Conditions isn't politically correct; however, doing so can lift you up when you are courageous enough to do so."

It's difficult for me to talk about some of the stories in my life without first addressing the perception of betraying others, a difficult lesson I learned after I wrote my first book. I had written a couple of short chapters in the 300-plus page book that had mentioned members of my family, who I later learned were upset over some of my revelations. I didn't necessarily think they were bad things, but it has definitely made me gun-shy when it comes to writing about other people.

So today, while I still encourage the writers that I coach to write about whatever is true to them, I also remind them about the importance of maintaining healthy relationships with their family and friends. Now, I think that's a really good thing, but oftentimes, it prohibits me from speaking about what is true to me. Therefore, although I am hesitant, I simply cannot tell the truth without letting you know about some of our shared business. And isn't that part of the reason you bought this book?

In my attempt to protect the innocent, I've changed some names and altered a few circumstances, but any of you who know me personally will know exactly who I'm talking about.

Anybody who has been in my life has been good people. And that's my disclaimer. If I loved them, that means they had something redeeming and beautiful about them. If I spent time with them or was in an intimate relationship with them, they were awesome when we connected. However, I admit that once I realized that the character flaws or bad habits existed, instead of paying attention to the red flags and disconnecting the relationships, I stayed when I shouldn't have in several cases. It's terrible to admit, but in my stubbornness to solve problems and fix things, I was foolish enough to think I could fix people, and I cannot. There are many of us who want to fix people. No one can. Some of my motivation came from wanting people to be patient with me as well. I'm fast, direct and have a generous streak, yet I'm no pushover, and I get frustrated over nonsense. Just like relatives, once I knew "they" were family, they were family, and I learned to deal. That translated into decisions I made about men I dated. This isn't a tell-all per se, but I want to own my part in this series as I talk about others as well as myself. I'm not trying to hurt or embarrass anyone.

But sometimes when we hold back, we miss our blessings. There have been numerous occasions where I have not said things because I wanted to save my face, or someone else's face, risking hurting my own self. When I think about my life, had I spoken up, stood back or really shared my true feelings at the time, those involved may have been spared pain or disappointment. One of the biggest inspirations for writing the *Clean Colored Girl Chronicles* is to give readers permission to tell what's true for them. Since I'm not a hypocrite, I can't coach anyone else without acknowledging my past and the incidents that have shaped my life and decisions. Hopefully those whom I love and who love me will understand.

Heart and Mind Dis-Ease

One of the reasons I want to talk about my life is because I think I've been through a lot and it has not been easy. But I'm still standing. And I feel that if I can stand and make it through, then so can you.

Relationships morph over time, especially when one person evolves and the other does not. They can also be affected by marriage, separation, divorce, time, age and health factors. Our biggest relationship influences are typically our nuclear family. We learn so much about how to operate by seeing what our parents and siblings do. We learn to comply, to compromise, to cooperate or to be combative based on early childhood experiences. Too many times we see our past through rose-colored glasses and don't acknowledge and deal with the scars, scabs and incidents that may have been detrimental to development. You all know, family can be something else!

My Early Life

I've always loved to read and somehow knew there was more to life than just going to work and coming home. I remember standing in the checkout line at the grocery store reading the little books within my reach. I especially liked the monthly horoscope books and *Reader's Digest*. Those publications gave me insight that there *was* more to learn than just what was in school, so I gobbled them up quickly in the few minutes I had with them.

To hear my parents tell it, I've always been quick. The night before I was born, my mom said she woke up feeling like she had butterflies in her stomach, so my dad started to time them. When they figured out her contractions were 20 minutes apart, dad called the doctor, who told them to get to the hospital. The funny part is, there wasn't enough gas in the car, so my dad funneled some from the lawnmower just to make sure they could get to the hospital. Then I guess I didn't want to stay "in there" because I was already pushing my way into the world by the time the doctor walked into the delivery room.

My dad has fond memories of caring for me as a baby, and mom says when I was first born, she got extreme headaches after delivery. It seems the medicine they gave her caused complications. My aunt cared for me while dad was at work, and at night, I slept in a drawer in their room, snug as a bug. Thinking of that makes me smile. My parents grew up together and married after my dad returned from

Vietnam. They remained married until I was two years old. My dad has remained in my life; however, since we never lived in the same city after they broke up, he wasn't a daily influence. A couple of years after their divorce, my mom married my stepdad and we, as a family, moved to St. Louis.

My mom is a talented, self-taught artist who did commercial art design while I was growing up. With my stepdad, we had a normal home life with rules, structure and dedicated family time. My stepdad started his career as an attorney in the criminal justice system and would tell us stories at the dinner table about juvenile delinquents, crimes committed by youth and the consequences of criminality. My younger brother and I never needed to be lectured about breaking the law because we knew we never wanted to end up like those children we had heard about.

From a young age, I was responsible for setting the table, some of the cooking, all of the dishwashing and getting my homework done before my eight o'clock bedtime. I was quick, so I always had time to help mom with art projects, help my stepdad fix cars in the garage or play with my little brother, with time to spare. At some point, my teacher told my parents that I often completed my work before the other students then would begin talking to them, distracting them from their work. My parents were proactive about me and my education, so around fourth grade, I was sent to counseling time that I had with my very own "Dr. Skiddis." I don't know what my parents told me about why I was going, but I happily enjoyed our time together, treasuring those times because she would give me little projects to do, she would share things with me, she listened well, and she was kind. I felt productive and comfortable with her. I admired her, and I think her presence in my life planted a seed within me of wanting to be like her in some way.

For the most part, my family life was normal, except when my mom and dad "talked" on the phone about me or about arranging visits to see my dad. They used me to communicate to each other: "Tell your mom this," "Let your father know that." It was frustrating because it would have been much easier for them to pick up the phone and speak directly. They refused to do so. As a result, I started picking up some of my negotiation and conflict management skills early on, though of course, I didn't realize it at the time.

Eventually, around my sophomore year in high school, my mom and stepdad divorced. Things were different around the house without his manly presence. Of course, a solid foundation had been laid, but not having him there every day allowed us to have less structure and rule enforcement. He was a phone call away, but as a teenager, I wasn't exactly "looking" for more structure, if you know what I mean. As I completed high school, I was very involved in activities and was a student leader, thriving, for the most part. Mom was actually my steady "weekend date" for a while. We used to watch *Dallas* and *Falcon Crest* on Friday nights then *The Love Boat* and *Fantasy Island* on Saturdays while playing gin rummy or two-handed spades for hours and hours. It was fun. Then as a junior, I started going to activities and on a few dates, in addition to getting my first job and, of course, my driver's license at 16 years old. On the nights I had to work, my brother had to do the dishes, but otherwise, I still had to set the table, do the dishes, do my homework and get my phone calls in all before 9 p.m., when I was supposed to be in bed on weeknights.

As we were getting older and mom lost me as her weekend date, she started dating too, but real dates. Until I started telling my stories, I didn't think about how my venturing out left a hole for her in her life and social calendar. She spent a lot of time home with her children before things changed.

College

This story is not necessarily mine, but I lived through it and believe it creates some context for my life as a young woman trying to be successful in relationships.

Let's talk about my mom. I'll start there. I love my mom. She is a beautiful person, a talented artist and was a great mom while I was growing up. We used to dye Easter eggs and decorate for Halloween, Thanksgiving and Christmas. We didn't have lots of big, big dinners because we didn't have a lot of family in St. Louis, but we always enjoyed the holidays because she made them special. However, when she and my stepdad divorced, my mom went through a transition. She was in her mid-30s, so she was younger than I am now, but she started dating. I guess her divorce was finalized when she was around 36 or 37, but she had never really dated. So she was out there, and she was very beautiful and young looking. Let's just face it: she was hot. So she would meet guys, and they just seemed to be up to no good. And it was hard because, at that point, I was in my teens; my mom was 21 years older than me, and I would meet these guys and just feel like they were bums and undeserving of her. And so it caused an issue because I wanted her to have a quality guy. My dad was quality, and my stepdad was quality. So she needed to have a quality guy, one of similar character, morals and principles, because that's what she was accustomed to.

Her after-divorce dating experiences took her and our little family through many, many ups and downs, which in hindsight, I'm sure all of us would change if we could. So let me go a little back through my mom's life and talk about why some of these things happened. My parents both grew up in Des Moines, Iowa, and they were each other's first love. My mom was 14, my dad was 16 when they were allowed to go to the movies together, only because their parents knew each other. By mom's sophomore year, she was allowed to actually date him. They got engaged during mom's junior year of high school. Dad went away to Vietnam, mom took some college classes, and when he came back, they got married. Neither one of them told me the story about how they broke up, but I heard about it later, and it made me sad. I think a lot of it had to do with when my dad had been away at war, my mom had been escorted to proms, graduation and things at my dad's insistence and in his absence. That ended up being an issue. When he came back, she was different and he was different too. They were married for five years or so. They stayed married long enough to have me and then got divorced when I was two.

Then, before we knew it, my mom had met my stepdad. She was working at a university. He was a grad student there, and they met, got married, and that's how we moved to St. Louis, where he is from. When they broke up, when I was about 15, my mom did kind of start dating, but she had had little or no experience with a single lifestyle. This was the mid '80s, she drove her Cadillac around, and she had this long beautiful hair; she was just a gorgeous lady. That's it. She spoke of feeling like she couldn't be herself in her marriages, like she was oppressed by the "husband rules" or their ways of treating her, which had been different than when they had been dating. She also said that parts of her died during her marriages as a result. Now that I'm older, I can relate to some of the things my mom had been going through at the time. Then, however, it was difficult for me and my brother to understand some of the decisions she was making. It was hard seeing her with people who were undeserving of her.

I've always had a lot of respect for my mom, and at the same time, our relationship has been strained a lot because we've had issues since I was a teenager. I was opinionated, and we would get into it about little things, resulting in arguments and stuff like that. And I never tried to be disrespectful, but ultimately, when I look back and think about some of the arguments we had had, or some of the incidents that had happened with us, other people would say, "Boy, I would never talk to my mom like that," or "This would never happen with my mom." I think what changed as I got older, and especially when I was in college, was that my mom started suffering from some health challenges. And some of her choices, the way she behaved and some of the things she did, caused me to feel like I needed to step up and almost take on the role of the parent. I'm not saying I actually had to become the parent. I just felt it was my responsibility to take care of my mom because of her health issues. I'm not saying it was right … it was just how I felt. So for most of my adult life, I have felt a certain responsibility to take care of my mom. And that has caused conflicts between us because even though she has these health challenges, she is still highly intelligent, highly independent and wants to do things her way. Well, I'm highly intelligent too, I guess, and highly independent, but I try to be reasonable. So oftentimes when we're together, we disagree. We can be together for a little while and things go smoothly, and then she'll say something and then I'll say something, and usually her feelings will get hurt, and it just goes from there. Many times I have to step back and keep my distance until things blow over. It's been hard. There have been many times when I've gone through breakups in my life or deaths of close friends but have not shared them with my mom because I felt like whenever I would talk to her about these types of things, it would exacerbate the situation by causing more drama, more pain, more explanation and more hurt feelings. My brother told me that I have a habit of picking up codependent relationships because I'm an enabler. At first, I laughed it off, but then I had to acknowledge that, to a certain degree, that was true. I just can't help myself because I really care about people. And the people that I love and care about, I want to do whatever I can to be supportive of them.

As I've said before, it's hard for me to go into too much business because I don't want to tell on other people. But I'm going to be as blunt as I can and maybe clean it up later. When I was a teenager, I saw my mom dating, and I saw some of the men she was hooking up with. It bothered me because I knew my mother was such a quality person. Later, she was diagnosed with depression. They did not classify it as a nervous breakdown, but she basically had a breakdown when I was a sophomore in college. She had been through so much. My belief is that it was a culmination of life as well as the individual she was dating at the time. I think he was the guy that took her over the edge.

They had been friends for a long time and had a good professional relationship. We knew all about him and that he and my mom were dating, but to his kids, they were just friends. At some point, something happened that caused him to overtly tell her that he didn't want anybody to know that they were dating. It was an interracial relationship, and I believe that was the only interracial relationship my mom had ever had. But when he rejected her like that, I think it sent her over the edge because of their professional relationship and the respect she had for him, not to mention her personal feelings for him. I got a call in my sophomore year of college, right before Christmas, from somebody. I don't remember who called me from St. Louis, but they said my mother was in the hospital and that it was pretty serious. I was in Columbia at Mizzou, which is an hour and a half away, getting ready to take my finals. When I got the news, I didn't have any choice but to pack up my stuff so I could head to St. Louis as my younger brother couldn't be home alone, and we had no idea how long she would be hospitalized.

I think classes were set to end in about 10 days. So I went to my counselor's office and the financial aid office to find out if I could complete some of my courses at UMSL, which is the St. Louis branch of the University of Missouri, and the following year return to Mizzou. I knew that I wanted to come back, and I also knew that I had to go home. After finals ended, my stepdad (who had remarried) came and got me. We took a U-Haul back to St. Louis, and I enrolled for the winter semester at UMSL, which would start after the holidays.

The Trumpet Player

My mom was in the hospital for a month. I made sure my brother got back and forth to school and had whatever he needed during that time. We went to the hospital regularly; uncomfortable little visits, we tried to be supportive, but it wasn't easy. I have no idea what happened over that holiday or where we even spent Christmas … we just made it through. I just remember that on my mother's birthday, a Tuesday at the end of January, she got out of the hospital and she wanted to "go out." This was 1990, and she decided to go to a popular St. Louis supper club in the Soulard District. She had been on all these medications, and I did not want her to go out. But she was unstoppable. She was going to go to that supper club. So I said if you're going out, I'm going too. Mind you, I was 19 (underage), but since I could not stop her, she could not stop me from going with her. We got to the spot, and of course, they were not carding because they were not expecting anybody young like me to walk in. I told her, "Don't tell anybody that I'm your daughter and it will be fine." She looked young, and of course, I was young, so we were both hot, in our own *Clean Colored Girl* kind of way. So we sit down and I ordered an Amaretto Sour, but I was really hawking her. I wasn't happy because it was a Tuesday and I had to be at school the next morning.

There was a band. In the band was a trumpet player. And baby, that trumpet player was just a-playin', and my momma was just a-singin', and then all of a sudden, he started playing to her and she started singing to him. When the set was over, she returned to the bar with me, and he soon followed. There was a lot of tee-tee and ta-ta, and ha-ha and hee-hee. At some point, she admitted that I was her daughter, to which he was not exactly surprised but surely not excited about. Yes, he played his instrument well; however, I was not impressed because he was a slick trumpet player. He knew that I knew it. He knew he would not win me over.

We closed down the bar. I was ready to go, and my mom said, "He's going with us ... him and his friend."

They are going to ride in the Silver Bullet, her Cadillac DeVille?

I said, "What? What do you mean they are going with us? Why are they riding with us?"

"Well, because he said his car is in the shop."

"Are you kidding me? These strangers, these grown men you don't know, are riding with us?"

She said, "Come on!"

I was pissed off. *How dangerous is this? If I wasn't here with her, would she have driven them by herself?* I was even more pissed.

The Trumpet Player was in the front seat with her, and his friend was in the backseat with me. As we were sitting there, the friend, who played the sax, had a Styrofoam cup in his hand. All of a sudden, I saw him going to his zipper. And I'm like, "What are you doing!?!"

Do you know he was getting ready to pee in the cup? I didn't know him, and he didn't know me, and he was getting ready to pee in the cup, getting ready to pull out his penis in front of me.

I said something else, and the Trumpet Player said, "Man, that's not cool. That's not cool." The sax player stopped; however, needless to say, that was strike number two.

We dropped off the sax player and then we went out to Richmond Heights, which is where this trumpet player lived. As we were pulling into the driveway, they explained to me that he did not live by himself, he lived with his momma! *Surely this disclosure took place between the two of them during the courting ritual, as added "security" that she would be safe taking him home.* I'm also thinking, *How in the hell was he planning to get home if we hadn't shown up???* Anyway, the only saving grace about him living with his mother was that she was in the same sorority that I was trying to get into. That made me feel as though he might have some type of redemptive qualities. *My young mind.*

We entered his mother's house and she was asleep, so I didn't meet her, but she had an extensive elephant collection, which I absolutely loved and admired for the first 20 minutes or so. However, I ended up sitting on the couch in the front room for a long time in his momma's house. *Strike three.* By then I was really pissed. It was almost three o'clock in the morning. All I could do was wait. I was absolutely stewing on that couch. *Will you please come on? I have school tomorrow! You don't even know that man! This is some BS! You aren't even supposed to be here. He doesn't deserve you. How can you be so shortsighted? Does he even OWN a car? I don't even stay out this late and I'm in college! What's taking so darn long?*

Eventually, finally, we left, and I was past the edge. I mean, I can't even tell you how upset I was at that point. Silence filled the Cadillac as we rode home in the wee hours of the morning. I didn't dare speak because in the midst of everything, I still remembered how fragile she was. *She should not have been out that night, period.* My anger was high, my patience was gone, and my heart began to break as I thought about the whole reason I was in St. Louis in the first darn place. My mom was sick. *Why in the heck am I on I-170, in St. Louis, heading home at four in the morning with my momma???*

The next day, I didn't speak to her about the night before, I just went to my classes. I got home before my brother and found a note on the kitchen table from my mom that said, "I'll be home later." When she came home, guess who was with her? The Trumpet Player. And when I say *with* her, I mean he moved from his momma's house to my momma's house. No car in sight. He was supposed to have this fancy little sports car that was in the shop. I never did see that car or any car, ever, just an old truck, much later. I heard the stories about his times in Los Angeles, playing in the band for some big Hollywood acts, but here he was back in St. Louis. *Why?* And he was living in *our* house.

When I saw him and he saw me, I knew it was going to be a problem. I could not believe that my mother would be that irresponsible coming out of the hospital, meeting him and making that type of a hookup. Talk about red flags, danger, etc. Hell had been brewing in the house for seven days. I was mad. I was upset. I thought it was disrespectful. I thought everything that was going on was just horrible, and I wished that I could have taken my brother and me out of the situation.

So my mom came home one day, and I was angry. She said something to me, I said something to her, and she snapped at me for being angry at her.

I screamed, "I left my life at college to come back here and try to take care of your household because you couldn't take care of it. And then you bring this bum into the house who doesn't have a job, doesn't have a car and is living off of you, and you think I'm going to be okay with it?"

No, I wasn't okay, and there was nothing okay about the situation. My mom's response was basically, *"You can leave."* That was early February. I was enrolled at UMSL, school had just started, and there were no choices. I couldn't go back to Mizzou that semester. I called a family friend and asked her if I could stay at her house until it was time for me to go back to Mizzou. She literally cleared out her basement where her son had previously lived and let me move in. I moved all of my stuff to her house. It was hard, but I really appreciated it. I didn't have any money and with what was happening, I don't think I had gotten a job yet, so it was good of her to let me stay. I continued to check in with my brother and did things with him, but I avoided *his* mother. *That's* how it started.

I made it through the semester, barely, with a GPA of 2.5. It was hard living in St. Louis instead of in a college town where everyone had studies and finals at the same time, so I was easily distracted. Between working, trying to study, dating (long distance since my boyfriend/eventual first husband was still in Columbia), living in a basement, dealing with feelings of rejection and trying to be "responsible," I had a lot on my plate. The summer was a bit easier. Thank goodness I was able to continue my paid internship at the

St. Louis Airport Marriott, through the INROADS program for talented minority students. The Saturday professional development sessions we attended, in addition to the corporate work environment, were just what I needed to get me and my feelings out of the soap opera my life had become. I went back to Mizzou in the fall, thank God! I rarely went back to St. Louis. I tried talking to my brother when I could, but he was a teenager and didn't really have too much to say. We loved each other and did what we both could to survive whatever circumstances we faced and supported each other the best way we could. To this day, we still do.

My mom and the Trumpet Player dated for about two years; there was all kinds of drama, and eventually, I learned that he used drugs. I had no experience in this area and neither did my mother, but that relationship cost her a lot of other relationships as a result. Dealing with him was a heavy price to pay for all of us.

Fast forward to my senior year of college. During my last semester at Mizzou, I had a problem with my boyfriend, who eventually became my husband. I was upset about what had happened and felt guilty about the incident, so I called my mom to confess to her and tell her what had happened because I thought our relationship was over. She sounded so sad when I finished my story, so I said, "I know it's pretty sad, but why are you sounding sadder than I am?"

And she said, "Oh, it's not that. I had an altercation with the Trumpet Player last night, and some stuff went down in the house. Your brother's at his dad's, and now I'm here by myself and I'm scared."

I was 120 miles away, it was raining outside, and I was afraid for my mom's life. While we were talking, my mom's phone clicked on the other end, and while I was on hold, I told my roommate what was going on. We weren't really the best of friends, we had kind of gotten thrown together as roommates, but she was decent enough. I said, "I need to go to St. Louis."

She said, "Well, you can't go by yourself. Let's take my car."

In the meantime, I was still holding for my mom, but she hadn't come back to the phone. That was 1992, so we were both on our house phones. I hung up and called her back, but she didn't answer, so I, too, was scared. We hopped in the car, got a ticket for speeding, but eventually arrived in St. Louis.

When we got to the house, it was storming and the screen door was locked, so I couldn't use my key. I knocked and knocked and knocked. She didn't answer the door even though I knew she was home. I started yelling, "Mom! Mom!"

"Jo, is that you?"

"Yes."

She unlocked all the locks and opened the door. When she saw me, she hugged me, burst into tears and said, "I thought you hated me. I thought you hated me."

"Of course, I don't hate you, but when you didn't click back over or answer the phone when I called back, I was scared that something happened to you. Why do you have all of the doors locked?"

"Because ... I'm afraid of him."

I was 22 and my roommate was about 20. It was time to rest, so I decided to sleep on the couch just in case *he* showed up. I wanted to be able to hear. My roommate slept in my brother's room, and my mom was in her room. At approximately three o'clock in the morning, I heard a noise. I got up, peeked outside and saw his truck. By that time, he must have been at the back door because I didn't see him, just the truck. I woke up my roommate and my mom, and we locked ourselves in the bathroom in my mom's room. As I was talking to 911, I realized Poncho, our American cocker spaniel, was not in the bathroom with us. My mom begged me not to get Poncho, but I said, "No, he will hurt him."

So I picked up the big glass bottle of Listerine to knock him over the head with if he busted in the door and ran out to get Poncho. Sure enough, as soon as I got back and locked us all in, we heard glass shatter. He broke in through the back door, looked around and tried to open my mom's bedroom door. When he realized it was locked, he kicked it in. We could hear his footsteps as he looked around the room. When he didn't see her, he ran downstairs. He looked around, came back upstairs, walked into my mom's room again and banged on the bathroom door three times.

Mom found her voice and said, "Harrison, what are you doing? What are you doing? It's Jo Lena. It's Jo Lena."

He was quiet but did not move.

I yelled, "Harrison!"

When he heard my voice, he immediately left the room and stormed out of the house.

It seemed like it was a long time, but it was probably only three to five minutes, and the police had not arrived. Another two or three minutes passed after he had left and we had not heard from them. The funny thing is that Poncho never barked, as if he knew our lives were in danger. So I picked up the Listerine bottle again and walked out of the bathroom door. Poncho was next to me, and we were ready. I got to the front door, and I saw the police across the street getting back into their car.

I yelled, "What are you doing?"

They said, "Oh, we didn't think anybody was home."

My roommate's car was in the driveway, and I can't remember if my mom's car was in the driveway or not, but I said, "He broke into our house and he just left."

Long story short, the police came in and noticed a blood trail where he had cut his hand on the louvers in our back door. They asked, "Did you actually see him?"

I said, "No. I saw his truck, and obviously, it was his voice and there's his blood. Isn't that enough?"

They said, "Well, since you didn't see him, we can't prove it was him."

My mom was all shook up. My roommate was all shook up. Poncho was quiet and close, all shook up. I was all shook up and pissed off. By this time, it was probably 4:15 a.m., when the phone rang. It could only be one person. The police told me to get him to confess.

I answered the kitchen phone while the officer listened on the cordless. "Hello."

"Heyyy, Jo Lena, let me talk to your momma."

"Let you talk to my momma??? Why did you break into our house?"

"Jealousy. Pure jealousy."

"That's no excuse. No! You cannot talk to my momma. I can't believe you broke into our house."

He asked again, and I denied him. I then hung up the phone since he had confessed. By that time, the police had dusted off everything and were getting ready to leave. There wasn't a lot of blood, but there was enough on the banister and floors for evidence.

The back door was busted. I can't remember who came over that morning, but somebody came over and boarded up the door. My roommate and I had to get back to school. My mother rode back to Columbia with us and stayed on campus for almost a week.

In one sense, mom loved being on campus because she was able to meet my friends and talk to my sorority sisters. But everything else in between was a blur. I think we were working on the Multicultural Extravaganza, a homecoming event I created during my freshman year, but I can't remember all the details. I was angry. I was upset. I was disappointed. I was scared. I was angry. I say that again because the night she met him I knew he was trouble.

The night the Trumpet Player entered our lives, everything changed. When I think about his friend and about him, and not having a car, it was all just bullshit. My mom was so vulnerable, and so … I don't want to say desperate because I don't think that's what she was. She had been cooped up. She had scars from her marriages. Her heart had been broken by the white guy. She thought she had recovered. She was ready to live. The Trumpet Player was charming. He was cunning and able to mesmerize her. In Hollywood, he had played with the Temptations, Commodores, Ray Charles and a host of other big-name groups. What we didn't know at the time was that he had burnt out, which was why he was back in St. Louis. More than likely, the entire time he was with my mom, he probably was on drugs. My mom was never addicted to drugs. But because she suffers from depression, she had been taking medication and also drinking alcohol with him. When you're drinking alcohol, even if it's a small amount and you're on medication for depression, that's a cocktail you don't want to mix. He didn't care about that. Because he was drinking, he wanted my mom to drink as well. And when you go to a club, what do you do? You drink. They had been playing this song for a couple of years.

Later on, I began to wonder why my mom was not talking to her best friend, Gloria, anymore. Several years later when I spoke with Gloria, she said that she had stopped dealing with my mom because of her drug habit. I was shocked. *Mom didn't have a drug habit.* I said, "What are you talking about? What drug habit?"

Gloria told me that the Trumpet Player had called her and said my mother was strung out on drugs and needed $2,000 to pay for something—the mortgage, the bills, some crazy something. Concerned, yet reluctantly, she gave him the money for my mom. She added that my mom never mentioned it or paid her back. He never paid her back. I cried, "Oh my God. My mother was not strung out on drugs and that did not happen. He stole from you."

Even to this day, I never told my mother that I had that conversation with Gloria, nor have we ever discussed the fact that the Trumpet Player was likely addicted to drugs. But I was glad that I met with her best friend again because I had missed her. She was like my aunt. I had grown up with her kids, who were like my older siblings, and I hadn't understood what was going on. I think I didn't mention it to my mom because by the time of this revelation, he was long gone and I didn't want to take her back to that time in her life.

That bum, here he goes again ...

I was reeling, spinning and hurting long after that conversation. I couldn't fathom the deceit and treachery of the Trumpet Player. It's as if something died in me that day. I lost a bit of hope and optimism as I gained a few new holes.

I shared that story because it shaped a lot of my thoughts, feelings and behaviors in regard to me, my identity and my perspective. Those experiences shaped my relationships and the way I saw people. I began questioning what love is and what love is not. They (the experiences and the people) had me jaded about how people behave when they love you and also how people lie when they don't love themselves and have no capacity to love you. We were messed up.

The Car Salesman

My mother had another relationship. This guy was handsome, and he was a car salesman, so he knew what to say and he knew what to do. He was tall, light in complexion and had a Jheri Curl. He had it going on. Think about Lionel Richie, El Debarge and Philip Michael Thomas. You know what I'm talking about. When she met him, everything seemed to be fine. There is a luxury car dealership in St. Louis called Premiere Motors, where he used to work. She felt good. He treated her well. They got along, with their outgoing personalities complementing one another. They seemed to have fun and had similar interests. He would frequently bring her rare, collectible items to add to her eclectic home décor, things which made her excited. She felt appreciated and loved. I was living in Los Angeles by then, so I wasn't around him very much, but I heard about their relationship when she and I spoke on the telephone. It was really encouraging to think that a quality guy recognized her for her brains, beauty and talent, treating her accordingly. For a time, I had stopped worrying about her, pleased that she was living her life joyfully.

Eventually, not too long after that, she found out that he was married. He told her that he was separated from his wife. Well, come to find out, he was still living at the house. I'm telling this story because once I found out that this man was still living at his wife's house, that was it for me. We had been cool, but when I found that out, it was upsetting, degrading and not okay. I would never be okay with that situation.

I have an issue when people cheat. You can say, "Well, I'm living with that person for convenience." If you're living in the same house, more than likely, you're in a relationship with them. More than likely, you're having sex with them. I don't care how late you're staying out. I don't care how much you're sleeping over, it's just not right, and I don't think any good comes from it. Eventually, it ended, but not before irreparable damage had been done. More holes.

Some of my mom's choices might have come from naïveté. Yet, wanting to be loved and having so much love to give but not finding that free expression to do it were not good for her. I can see that she was kind of green in some areas. While she was living a married life, those men were out whoring around. They knew the game and knew what to say to draw her in. The Trumpet Player and the Car Salesman are just prime examples of men who caused a huge rift in our family because I was angry, judgmental and affected as a young woman, seeing the effects they had on my mother.

Now that I'm older than my mom was when she was making those decisions, I have much more empathy and compassion for what she went through and for the choices she made. I get it. I, too, have fallen in love with guys who were not available—be it emotionally or physically. Holes, holes and more holes.

Family Dynamics

Mother/Daughter Dynamic

As long as mom is still on this earth, I will feel a sense of responsibility toward her. However, if I'm going to be completely honest, I'm angry with her every single day as well. She's been a smoker since before I was born—so, for nearly 50 years. As she has developed physically limiting health challenges, I have wanted her to stop smoking, but she won't. That makes me boil because it only makes her more ill. Yet, what can I do? She's not going to stop (though she plans to), and I'm not going to stop being upset by her choice (though I probably should). We all have our addictions and predilections. Hence, we get to part of my issue with love and relationships—loving someone despite what they do. In the case of my mom, it's the right thing to do because she's my mother. In the case of intimate relationships, some people just don't deserve a reserved, precious space in my life. Instead of taking my time, testing them out or releasing them when they revealed their true selves, I tried to work with them, making excuses and ignoring issues rather than facing problems. It doesn't work. Though those relationships have passed, I am still my mother's daughter. Mom and I have a pretty good understanding now. Our relationship is much more important than our differences. We love each other and have found ways to listen and share without ruffling each other's feathers too much. I really appreciate and respect the woman she is and her dedication to doing her best as a person and as a mother.

Father/Daughter Dynamic

I love my biological father. I made a decision when I was 27 to have him in my life despite the fact that we really didn't get along. I know he loves me, but I don't think he likes me very much, at least, when I speak out. He's told me many times that I'm "too strong," and he has in his own way attempted to "break me down" to build me up. That probably works if you grow up in the same household, but not when your parents divorce when you are two years old. He's of a different generation and sees things way differently than I do. If I hold my tongue, he's fine, so I've learned to do that around him, for the most part. So no, I don't know about the comfort and security of being "a daddy's girl." It's not my experience. I know I'm being a little coy, but this is not the book where I'm going to get into our relationship deeply. So, I will say this: He's a Taurus and I'm a Leo. If you know anything about zodiac signs, then apply all the stereotypes you know into that statement and you have a homemade showdown at the *O.K. Corral*!

My Other Dad

As I mentioned before, I grew up in the household with my stepfather, who has been my dad since I was nearly four years old. That's over 40 years of guidance, wisdom and love. My teenage years were a little rough, but once he and my mom divorced, our relationship became easier, especially around my senior year in high school. One day we had a talk. We talked about things that had happened, didn't happen, what he thought, believed and felt. In the car that day, I learned that men can and do love deeply; that he was extremely hurt by the divorce; that he really loved me and my brother; and that he was not going to stop being my dad. He opened his heart to me, and that helped me to know that one day a man who loved me intimately would do the same. He's allowed me to work with him, and he's taught me a lot. He's honest, though not judgmental, and we get along well, though he's totally reserved and I'm not so much so!

Headstrong and Determined

For most of my life, once I made up my mind to do something, I stuck to it. That's great when it comes to work-related tasks and duties. I'm pretty reliable and considerate of people's needs. I like serving. However, in relationships, it's not one of the best ways of being. I didn't pump the brakes when I could have or should have. I liked who I liked, I decided to be loyal, and I put up with some things out of foolishness, naïveté and plain ole love—my concept of love, at least, based on my *Broken Conditions*. So, when you read some of these stories, you may "worry" about me, but I don't want you to. I'm dynamic and blessed to be resilient. With each choice, I learned something, picked up new skills and made it through, at times, improving in the process. At 47 years old, I'm much wiser about my choice of mates and about my own behavior. Not a master, but wiser. However, there are many experiences and adventures between what happened back then and today …

He Wasn't My Husband

"Once we get caught up in sin, we contaminate every other relationship we are involved in when not cleaned from the last. The only common denominator in what went wrong was you... God blocks it (the next relationship) because he wants to clean you up before letting you walk into another relationship with dirt under your feet, nails and whatever is inside. We have tried to clean up our sin on our own, but we cannot do that on our own because we are not equipped. God doesn't have to search for the proper cleaner. When we sin and when we fall, all God has to say is Jesus, "'I'ma need your blood on that."
– Pastor John Gray, The Cost of Cleanup Sermon,
September 2017

Lord, my concerns have turned to worry. I feel consumed with guilt, shame, confusion, hurt and anger. I know my past is haunting me, and my thoughts are allowing emotional strongholds to keep me bound. This does not serve me at all. My feelings stem from my decision to get involved with MC. The day I met him, it's like the sky had opened and the water started flowing! He was handsome, sweet, kind and a good listener. We chatted, evidently, for over an hour about life. Toward the end of our chat, I found out he was in an unhappy marriage—but married nonetheless. Once he told me that, I immediately went into "coach" mode and asked him about the relationship, had he tried certain things, and if he was willing to do what he could to keep it. He was discouraged and felt that, ultimately, it was over. It was just a matter of time and planning before he would leave. In that moment, I genuinely wanted what was best for him. Within family dynamics, I felt it best to work it out if possible. But he had the second half of his life to live, and it didn't make any sense for him to stay in a broken situation, being stuck if he really knew it was over. Eventually, we were interrupted and parted ways, as he had another engagement.

Instead of simply walking away from our conversation and leaving it there, I contacted him the next day on Facebook and sent the picture we had taken. At the time, I hadn't realized we had taken two pictures, and the second was so intriguing. He looked enamored, and I was happy. His response was to thank me for the picture and the encouragement I had given him—about marriage and his life. From our first conversation, we had hit it off. I mean, we were laughing, joking, texting and exchanging heartwarming pleasantries. It was what I had dreamed of, or so I thought. As our talks progressed, there was someone else in my life who was lurking around. He was okay, but I was a bit lonesome. Since MC was quite busy with work and life, I thought giving the other guy the time of day would be a good thing. In the end, the other guy, being an arrogant ladies' man who simply got on my nerves, highlighted how much I preferred MC.

Therein lay the problem. Things were getting more serious—not in the physical sense, but in the emotional sense. We were in constant contact, and I was falling deeply for him. I was also strongly conflicted because I didn't just want to text and talk or see each other just to have sex; I wanted the whole package—something he was well aware of and, for a time, acknowledged being willing to pursue. However, I am not cut out to be a side chick, and I was freaking out because I didn't want to share and I didn't want to be strained or restrained. I wasn't a conformist, and it wasn't fun. The deeper our communication got, and the couple of times we were together, it just felt comfortable—right—like we had known each other forever. He even said that being there with me was like he had just come "home" from a trip. I believe these exchanges and feelings were genuine and mutual.

Yet my prayers and thoughts were on what I couldn't ignore—he was not free. He was not divorced and, at that point, had not filed for divorce. Granted, he acknowledged that he loved her as a person but was no longer *in* love, and he was out all the time … working or just hanging out, doing everything except being home. And in the midst of all this, when we were supposed to get together, for dinner or simply to meet, several times, he couldn't make it. Something literally came up. And when I say this, I'm not speaking of him making excuses; I'm speaking of actual occurrences that prevented us from being together, though we both longed to be. Since I was not in my element, I was trying to conform and be patient with him, trying not to be upset or feel rejected because I felt his intentions were in the right place. In the space of nearly four months, I waited nearly 10 times for no-shows. The last significant one, he simply texted me that perhaps it was too stressful for both of us, and that he was tired of disappointing me. Honestly, I was relieved. I didn't think I could take one more night of beating myself up for allowing this situation and encouraging it to continue.

I cared, I felt love for him, and I enjoyed the way he treated me in the beginning. This goes to what I have said before—I didn't put on the brakes at any time when I consciously knew I should have. The few friends who knew the situation supported me by being honest with me—knowing full well, like I did, that it wasn't a healthy situation and it wouldn't end well. In the meantime, we stopped and started and then almost completely stopped communication. However, my feelings still flared up, and I reached out to him. During this period, I met other men; I was in a "hot stage"—not hot in the pants, but for some reason, I was attracting men without effort during this time. So, if I could have done what people say you should do and "fill the space" with others to take my mind off MC, I likely would have been okay. But I couldn't even do that. He was the one. Not them. In one of our last, most significant conversations, he had told me that he found me to be caring but also overbearing and felt I was trying to fix him. It got to the point where the only contact we had was when I reached out. Most of the time, he would reach back. There was a period of about one week when he was supposed to be in touch to see me and he didn't. That told me it was really over … and I could kind of deal with that part. I only wanted to be with him if he wanted to be with me, but there seemed to be something else going on, and since he didn't say what it was, that feeling of needing to know was bigger than anything else.

Then one night, it occurred to me that something was off. There was something I needed to know—something I had been missing. So I went to a place I figured he would be … and he was. And I saw something I didn't expect. He had another woman there—and not his wife. I had, by that time, had three shots of premium tequila and was more than shocked. I thought his distance was giving him a chance to change his situation and not do wrong by my desires. I got it all wrong. Just as I had entertained suitors and such, he had clearly done the same. And this woman was his woman, at least, that's what she said when she told me he was her man. And that was before he told me to leave him alone, that he wasn't dealing with me. It was a terrible situation in a public place … a public place I should have never been and in a situation I had caused because I would not leave well enough alone. Something inside me drove my need to know, to have to get down to the bottom of his behavior. Something inside me put myself and him in a compromising position—one from which we would never recover.

As I type this with that sick, sinking feeling in the pit of my stomach again, I am admitting to myself, to you and to God that I have a problem letting go that is far more serious than MC or any particular man, person or situation.

Every single day that I called myself "wanting him" was every single day that I was struggling, wrestling with myself about why, even though we had such a natural connection, I was tormented about being with him. He was a married man and not married to me. I did not want that. I knew I deserved more, and I knew it was not right. Surprisingly, even though I had tried to "help him" sweeten things with his wife in the beginning to see if the relationship could be salvaged, I didn't feel guilty about her. That was probably one of the biggest signs that I was totally off course in my life. I had gone into unchartered territory, and there I stayed, compromised and compromising. I don't blame him; he could have really taken advantage of me—my feelings and vulnerable state toward him—but he didn't. Of course, I wish he would have just told me flat out, in that last week, what the deal was because I could have handled it. But since he didn't, I did what I had learned to do—kept digging, persevering and needing to find a resolution.

This is not about him, it's about me because I can't speak about what drove him to all of his choices, but I will say, I still care. I am praying to become unattached to him and to all toxic relationships in my life. The challenge is that the root of my love life appears to be toxic. It's what I had learned: Don't give up on people, don't stop loving them when they do something wrong and don't upset the apple cart too much if you want them to stay around. I learned this from my relationship with my father. And as late as the spring of 2017, I was still trying to conform to that kind of love … and it has almost killed me. My soul has been dying because I haven't felt like I could have what I wanted and haven't felt like I have made the types of choices that could provide the stable, healthy relationship intended for me because I have been caught up in entanglements. I noticed that almost every time I reached out to MC after a stretch apart was when something negative had happened and I needed some type of comfort. That's unhealthy but true. I wasn't turning to food, drinking or drugs, but I needed acknowledgment and not to continue feeling alone in the world. See how sick that is? He was someone else's husband. And trust me, this is not about a sexual tryst, because that wasn't our deal. Connection and emotional ties to someone, especially when both are not in a good place, can be dangerous and consuming. At first, we were refreshing to each other, but then my guilt got the best of me and I spazzed out. That became tiring and unappealing to him. And amid all of this? I believe it was God who protected me as I struggled, failing a big test, but pushing me forward nonetheless.

Every single day I was in my Bible ... actually, in my Bible app on my phone. I read the daily Scripture and then devoured the Bible plans. I was praying for me, for him, for help and, ultimately, for what I wanted—my wholeness and my own significant relationship, one of which I could be proud. I wanted to be able to walk in confidence, knowing that I was being who I am and behaving in a manner that I would expect of myself and that God would expect of me. I was past desperate—I didn't feel that—but I wanted real love and to know that I mattered and how much I mattered. No one else could give that to me. The experience proved to me that it didn't matter about MC and his marriage or choices; while I had cared for him, I was still open to the right situation, and if someone free would have come along whom I was actually interested in, I would have jumped over there, since MC and I didn't really have a leg to stand on. My fight was my internal battle, and it could not and would not be solved by blaming anyone in the past for the ways I had felt hurt, mistreated, abandoned or rejected. And there we get to the heart of my issue—rejection.

In my life, I have had this problem. I literally learned to fight people to love them.

I have a couple of other issues too: Relationships and certain associations have been distractions to me because I can't balance everything and still excel in all my endeavors. So work can be going good, then here comes a man. Or I need work and here comes a client whose life, experiences and emotional states become so consuming to me that I have gotten sucked into their world and their drama, leaving me to claw my way out. Finally, no matter how much I try, even though I know he loves me, it seems I will never please my father. I feel oppressed when I'm around him; although I know I love him, he's probably never going to change.

Not letting go. That's the problem. In all of it, I truly am the living, breathing Absolute Good Resilience Coach, recovering after something bad happens, but like the Israelites wandering around Mount Sinai for 40 years on an 11-day journey, this Clean Colored Girl is worn out! No more doing things the way I want to for the moment because the moment never satisfies. No more giving into flattery or craziness because I feel a little lonely or I'm concerned about my bank account/paying my bills. When I was young, I didn't settle, and now that I'm older, I surely can't settle. In my heart I know what I want—but what I learned in the entangled affair with MC is that I cannot trust my heart!!! And if someone tells you to trust your heart, don't do it.

The heart wants what it wants and cannot reason. It follows the dominate thoughts and sinks to the lowest levels of lust, desire, deception and all manner of debauchery. It's important to have a compass to guide yourself—so even when off course, having and reading the compass and actually following the compass are the only ways to get back to center, or at least on a forward-moving path. For me, without reading my Bible, I would likely not be in my right mind. I mean that. It's easy to sway to the left, right or into the arms of the wrong person or situation.

Being my age and not having a personal relationship with a child or mate, and complicated relationships with my parents, causes me sadness and grief at times. Other times, I feel impatient. Still at other times, when I see some of the problems and issues people have to deal with, I'm relieved to not be in those situations. I don't mean to sound ungrateful. I just think those holes are terrible and have prevented me from creating the deep ties that are possible when one is truly shining from within. I do believe there is something to the Law of Attraction … a lot of something. Broken people attract broken people. Radiant people attract the same. I ebb and flow and know that I'm a good woman, but instability has been one of my vulnerabilities. Part of it is about creativity and independence, and part of it is about making sound business decisions that are not tied to my heartstrings, which is kind of hard for me when I feel my purpose is to be a servant.

Hence, I am not qualified to make decisions on my own. I will mess up by myself. So, calling on the Lord, my God, is what I must do. It's what I do. It's also what I must consistently do when in the middle of a mess so that I don't continue gravitating to or attracting that mess. Learning to define boundaries and keep them there is a process—one I've failed miserably at in the past. But … I chose not to be limited to my past. Intuition served as a warning sign! At my core, I knew what I wanted and trusted God until

I could begin to trust myself to live in that truth. Those innate feelings kept me uncomfortable until I stopped fighting and was released.

This Affirmation Works!

I claim the exit from my life of all those who are not for my highest good; they fade from my life and prosper somewhere else.

"I waited patiently for the Lord; he turned to me and heard my cry. He lifted me out of the slimy pit, out of the mud and mire; he set my feet on a rock and gave me a firm place to stand." – Psalm 40:1

Looking for Love

How many times do we find ourselves looking for love in all the wrong places? Too many! For me, I have so much love to give, I want somebody who can appreciate and respect that love. I've always liked men in suits, cuff links and nice shoes—you know, well-dressed, chivalrous men. When a man is in a nice suit, it can be hard to tell when he is a slick guy; it's just hard to know. You don't see the real person. And when I say slick, I don't think anybody I've seriously dated has been a bad guy because, if they were, I would not have dealt with them for any time.

One of the best guys was my college sweetheart. We got married, I moved to Los Angeles, and he joined me in L.A. after he graduated with his master's degree. But as young people grow up, they grow apart, and that's what happened to us. He was an elite, world-class athlete and talented hardworking man who didn't know much about being married at the time. I respect him, yet we were not suited for a life together. We didn't have a lot of drama or changes, but our personalities and interests weren't compatible enough to keep a marriage bond. We are in touch occasionally and continue to root for the best in each other's lives.

After we broke up, I mostly ate grilled chicken from my favorite spot, *El Pollo Loco*, and I spent many hours working out in the swimming pool doing water aerobics, which resulted in a nice, svelte, glistening brown body with even tighter thighs and legs, a flat stomach (something I hadn't seen in years) and a very nice upper body. I also switched jobs. During our marriage, I had been the marketing coordinator for a transportation planning and traffic engineering firm located on the Santa Monica Pier. From my office, I could see the ocean. I was making a nice salary, but after working through the sadness of divorce, I was bored and ready for something new. When a friend invited me to a networking meeting, I took my résumé, just in case. Though the meeting turned out to be about multilevel marketing, I met a friend of that friend, who had been wrangled in like me. We got to chatting, and he told me that he worked as a contemporary marketing team (CMT) representative for Anheuser-Busch. His boss was looking for a new team member, and he thought I would be perfect. I whipped out my résumé and the rest was history! I got the job as a CMT rep and went from the office into the field. Though I didn't drink beer, I was representing Budweiser, managing Bud girls, building the brand and hosting parties for strangers and friends in bars and clubs from Beverly Hills to Compton. It was so much fun! A big change from corporate life, I was enjoying my new job and the perks that came with it and my new life.

Transitioning into being a single woman was kind of weird because I had been connected to my ex-husband for eight years. Well, when I was minding my own clean colored business, attending a house party with some friends, I met Evan. He was a beautiful, caramel genius who was a corporate accountant by day and an interesting, car-collecting, organized but rough-around-the-edges guy from Alta Dena, a small suburb north of L.A., at night. We clicked, and that was it. Oh my goodness! He was unlike anybody I had known. I loved his intelligence, attention to detail and his white '64 Chevy Impala. I found it hard to believe that cars could be that old and still look that good, 30 years later, mostly because of the Southern California climate. We had some amazing times, taking long drives along the Pacific Coast Highway, smoking cigars in the backyard, playing dominoes and going to house parties, a favorite pastime back then. I was hooked on Evan, and he was into me, but not fully. He still had a thing for his ex-girlfriend. She didn't live in the city anymore, but she had broken his heart, and he never let himself get over it. That was okay with me because I couldn't do anything about it. We were friends, buddies, and we enjoyed each other's company. We ended up dating for over a year before parting ways, amicably. At the point that happened, I was about to enter into the "real" dating world …

When I was living in Los Angeles, I had a lot of first dates. If my date wasn't able to hold a good conversation, there was no chemistry, or he never said something that really sparked my interest, we didn't see each other again. That may sound superficial, but I was in Hollywood, after all. There were some fine men in Hollywood. I was pretty fine back then myself—thin, and I honestly didn't know how pretty I was; I just thought I was regular just like everybody else. I wasn't, by L.A. standards. I wanted somebody to spend time with me and enjoy my company. And I think when they met me, they thought one thing, but when they got to know me, it didn't quite gel. I was okay with that because I was more than a nice rack with strong legs and a winning smile. I was a Midwesterner. My values were a little different, and quite frankly, I was serious, had great careers, worked hard and went to church. When it was time to play and have fun, I played, enjoyed being a woman and having fun. However, if we couldn't make it past the first date, they didn't experience that part of me.

Wanting to continue excelling in my career, as Anheuser-Busch was ending the CMT positions, I started doing double duty. I did promotions in the evening and became promotion director at KACE Radio. It was exciting, lucrative and right up my alley. I was able to do radio giveaways: Easter egg hunts, CD and movie release promotions and, of course, concert giveaways. I had the means, access and ability to go where I wanted, and of course, I didn't want to do it alone. Along the way, I met a few intriguing guys who I dated more than once, casually. Yet I didn't want to be associated with too many people. Besides, I have traditionally been a one-man-at-a-time kind of clean colored girl. About two years later, the radio station was purchased and closed by another big company as they were consolidating and changing formats. Fortunately, we had plenty of notice, and I was able to secure another opportunity immediately.

Eventually I met and dated Hershel, the Hollywood music guy, for a of couple years. He was from Chicago and was super cool. When I began doing marketing, promotion and events for Courvoisier Cognac as the brand ambassador for the West Coast, he helped me with my promotions and connected me with many contacts. One of the most memorable times we had together was when I hosted a party at the Playboy Mansion. Hershel got to take pictures with a few of the Bunnies, the ice sculpture was gorgeous, the place was amazing, and the product launch went well. He was my ride or die for a time. We got along very well, but I wasn't into him like I needed to be to sustain a longer-term relationship. To this day, we remain friends.

Before I left L.A., I also dated Donnie, the DJ, for about a year. He taught me high-level negotiation skills and worked with me to build the Courvoisier brand even more, through partnerships, concerts and parties. Our biggest mistake was going into business together. That killed our relationship as he made some bad business deals; one of his biggest ventures was shut down right before it was supposed to happen because of 9/11. He had planned a huge

NYC concert at the Coliseum for the end of September. When the Twin Towers went down, our lives changed—and the concert disappeared too. There was no recovering the investment and no rescheduling. I walked away from him brokenhearted, because I had really liked him, and with a tax write-off because he didn't repay my personal investment. That stung. We were out of touch for over a decade because he didn't make an effort to rectify the friendship, the relationship or the outstanding investment. I got hustle and grit out of that relationship. My enthusiasm for being in Hollywood, with the glitz, glamour and glass houses, started to wane after that; however, I wanted to do something more meaningful with my life, and I wanted to be around people who were real, not fronting.

I started feeling like I wanted to create events in people's lives, not just create events. I loved marketing, promotion and events—and that's how Absolute Good started and grew. During the Anheuser-Busch years, I learned how to build brands from the best and how to manage promotional models and campaigns. While at the radio station, I learned how to create campaigns, appeal to people's needs and manage a staff of creative people who enjoy life. When working with Courvoisier, I created my own temporary staffing agency, employing, training and teaching promotional models to educate consumers on our brands, while helping them supplement their pockets, tuition fees and life dreams at a time when all of us were seeing stars, literally. At one point, I had over 50 people working on my team throughout southern and northern

California. My time in Los Angeles was THE BEST. I had great friends from college, new friends from L.A. and fellow transplants who were making it in the City of Dreams. And then, like the song, I felt like leaving on the *Midnight Train to Georgia* as the facade faded and purpose drove me more than passion. My divorce had been made bearable by years spent healing, learning and studying at my Los Angeles church home. That experience had awakened me to my calling to reach and teach people from my education, career, experiences and heart, and I knew it was time to answer the call. I had begun to listen and yearn for more. I packed up my things and moved around a little bit, as I began doing public speaking and learning to become an effective facilitator and soft-skills trainer. Suitcases and traveling could have been my middle name!

Now I'm going to fast forward to a couple of significant relationships in the 2000s that really shaped my life.

Aunt Josie

I've been fortunate to have some amazing people who helped shape my life and who have loved me unconditionally. One of those people was Aunt Josie. She was my stepdad's sister and a fellow Leo lady. My Aunt Josie was a gem. She was a dedicated member of her Catholic church for over 30 years, and she always spoke up for people. In the 1980s, Aunt Josie became the first Black female from her district to be sworn in as a delegate for the state of Maryland (a Maryland state representative). As a result, she helped to shape laws that still affect citizens of the state today. After serving her term, she went on to work for the governor's office and then to spend many crucial years as an advocate for children while working with the Maryland Infants and Toddlers Program. Despite the busyness of her career, she always made time for family.

I lived in Portland, Oregon, for about a year and then moved in with Aunt Josie, just outside of Washington, D.C. This was much different than living in L.A. for those eight years. I was traveling as a contract training consultant and was rarely home during the week. Moving to the East Coast gave me a chance to explore and get experience and exposure to the fast-paced lifestyle and people. I loved the meaningful work, the travel and coming home to Aunt Josie after teaching classes and taking trains, planes and rental cars almost daily. We had a blast whenever we were together. Aunt Josie was the role model I think all kids deserve—an adult who loves them, cares for them, shares with them, teaches and guides them, and who does not have to deal with all of the discipline and pressures of parenting. Having lived on my own most of my adult life, I felt loved when she prepared my favorite meals—including collard greens, turkey wings and cabbage. We so enjoyed long chats about the previous week's adventures while eating our food.

That woman showed me that I could travel, write, be nice and have fun while helping people. She taught me by showing me because that was her life; she lived that way. She always liked fancy, girly things, the latest trends and color. She used to be a plus-sized model in her spare time. She was fluffy, fabulous and fun. But I want to be specific about why every child should have an "Aunt Josie." While we were growing up, Aunt Josie sent cards for every occasion—St. Patrick's Day, Easter, Halloween, Thanksgiving—and "she" was usually the real gift at Christmas because she would come back to St. Louis to visit us! With Aunt Josie, we found loving tenderness and fun-loving guidance. She cared for us, groomed us and would write long, handwritten letters filled with pictures of historic monuments from around the world when she traveled to see them.

As a wife, she loved her mate, although her marriage to Uncle Leonard lasted only five years. He died of complications due to diabetes. During their short time together, he was her number one supporter. He built up her courage and confidence to leave her hometown of St. Louis, and she allowed him to "lead her to victory" in the campaign. He also encouraged her to make a positive impact on her nieces, nephews and children around the world. She listened to him; he loved her. He was assertive and sometimes loud. She was sweet, appropriately reserved and always appreciated for her contributions. We lost Aunt Josie unexpectedly in 2010, and I still miss her dearly. However, I treasure her memory and the way she lived her life. I knew if Aunt Josie could travel the globe, help people and still enjoy life, I could too.

King Tut and Nathan

In late 2006/early 2007, I was very single, doing great, traveling around the world conducting training sessions. By that time, I had been to England, Scotland, Northern Ireland and to almost every state. I usually taught for one day then left the city when I was on the East Coast. However, I was so excited because Philadelphia was one of my stops, and I was going to be there for a couple of nights, which would allow me to see the Tutankhamun (King Tut) exhibit was at the Philadelphia Museum. I taught my leadership class that day, and as soon as it was over, I walked from my hotel to the museum, which was literally a block away! I saw King Tut and the entire exhibition. I was just on a high when I left because I had experienced that history, perfectly content, by myself.

When I walked back into the hotel, the concierge, who had spoken to me on my way to the exhibit, said, "How did you like the exhibit?"

"Oh, it was wonderful." And I started telling him all about it because, who else was I going to tell?

Meanwhile, I had not really been paying attention, but the concierge had also been talking to a guy before I walked in the door. And after this guy heard all of my enthusiasm and excitement, he said, "Well, hello," in an almost Barry White melodic tone.

"Hello."

"My name is Nathan, and I'm a publisher."

"A publisher? What do you publish?"

He said such and such magazine, and I said, "Oh, okay. I'm Jo Lena. I'm a trainer, and I'm here to teach some leadership classes."

I noticed the concierge had gone. The introduction had been made, I was exhilarated from the exhibit, Nathan was friendly with a kind smile and beautiful voice. We sat and talked for an hour or so. We had a great conversation. He lived in Toronto, Canada, but was originally from the Caribbean and was here on business.

At the end of our conversation, he asked, "What are you doing tomorrow?"

"I'm teaching, and you're welcome to come to my class if you'd like."

"Would you like to go to lunch?"

"Okay, but since I don't know what time exactly I will send the class to lunch, would you like to come to my class and we'll leave together?"

"Sure," he replied with a nice, toothy grin.

Eventually (not on time), he showed up, and we went to lunch. Immediately after that class, I had to leave for the next city, but he gave me his phone number, and we talked for the next couple of days.

At that time, I was living in the Washington, D.C., area. We stayed in touch over the next month or so, and eventually, I took the train to Toronto and met him. I had my own hotel room, and we just hung out in Toronto for a couple of days. He was very nice and showed me the sights of the city but not his car. I can't remember his excuse about the "missing" car, but we were taking public transportation. Toronto is similar to New York, where public transportation is the norm, so I wasn't really concerned. I met a couple of his friends. It was kind of interesting because I remember at some point, and I'm sure it was before I went to Canada, I had asked him how old he was and he had told me a number, but I felt that he was older than what he had said. I remember thinking, *Why would he lie?* I mean, I knew he was older than me, and I guessed that there was probably a 15-year age difference, but I let it go. I mean, I was in my late 30s, so I wasn't too young for an older man, in my opinion. We continued to talk, I ended up going to Toronto again, and he came down to the U.S., at least once, and we ended up dating.

I moved to Toronto and lived there for almost a year. Of course, during that time, the nonexistent magazine, with only a cover, ended up becoming an actual magazine by the time I became the senior editor and hired a graphic designer, wrote a bunch of the copy and got other writers to write copy. The whole experience was amazing. Now, mind you, I had never in my wildest dreams thought about publishing, editing or writing anything. I had been an Honors English student in high school, but I had never thought about writing professionally.

The magazine turned out beautifully in terms of design and content. However, there was a huge problem; we ordered the wrong binding for the magazines. We had about a week or two before the launch, and when the 2,000 magazines came back, they looked extremely unprofessional because they had been stapled instead of glued. In hindsight, it probably wasn't as bad as we thought it was then, but it wasn't the product we had wanted. We had to do a reprint to launch the magazine and appeal to the big-dollar advertisers. Because of the disaster, we could only order 200 copies because he had spent about $6,000 to get the first round printed. We had no more budget. I worked some miracles, and we got the updated magazines printed in the United States for far less. I went home, picked them up and brought them back from Maryland. We gave them out sparingly because we were up a creek. He was responsible for the advertisers, and I was responsible for the content. Somehow, the paying advertisers weren't really cutting checks, and he wasn't really pounding the pavement or aggressively making phone calls.

How did I get caught up in all of this? What can I say? I'm a project person ...

I had gotten caught up because I like to help people, and I like projects. In the past, some of those people became projects, and in the context of relationships, that's not healthy, I know.

He paid all the bills for the luxurious 23rd-floor, one-bedroom loft overlooking the Toronto Harbourfront Centre. We went shopping weekly at the huge farmer's market, took the trolley wherever we went and enjoyed the bar and social life of our upper-crust building. I wasn't really into him romantically, but he was a good companion, we got along well, he didn't pressure me, and we were working on our project! Never saw a car, by the way.

We started working on the second edition of *our* quarterly magazine, and it was going well. We retained the graphic designer, found a new photographer, and eventually, the magazine just got and looked better and better. Well, about that time, staff and consultants started telling me that their checks were bouncing, which made me start wondering what was going on with his finances. I was invested, and I was nervous. I felt like he was betraying me and a lot of loyal, hardworking, creative people. Besides, I had found my niche and was loving the new world of publishing. I had to get into detective mode.

Long story short, he had lied about his age; he had lied about his finances; he had lied about his ex-wife, who turned out to be his ex-girlfriend and his son's mother. Everything was a lie. He was an old, flat-broke swindler, borrowing money from his friends based on my results and leadership with the magazine—knowingly writing bad checks and overdrawing accounts just to pay the hefty bills. I wasn't going to stand for it. I had discussions with those affected and forced him to make good on the outstanding payments. Before, I hadn't been snooping, looking or really worried about his age or money. He was taking care of the basics, and I was giving him grace, though losing patience about his lack of advertising sales. A male friend felt I should have stopped after I discovered there was no magazine. He's absolutely correct. I didn't see it that way then, and I doubt I would have listened.

My name was on the line. You know how somebody you're with introduces you, and you can feel that they're looking at you, wondering why you're with that person. That's what seemed to be going on. It was a mixed bag, like people were almost elated to meet me. It was like, wow! I thought it was because I was American. But that wasn't the case. It was because they could tell that I had a little integrity about myself, and they were kind of encouraged that he had made a sure enough upgrade. They were wondering what was going on with him. They must have thought I had money (which I did not). He was a charming older guy, who obviously hadn't been about much before I had arrived, which of course, I did not know. When I found out he was bouncing checks, I was very upset because that was not okay. I felt betrayed, angry, ashamed, embarrassed and trapped. Here I was, living in another country with that hustler. New holes.

Within a week of those revelations, I was on the phone talking to my brother; that was the first time we had talked in a while. We spoke for nearly three hours. I told him what was going on, and he said, "Jo, you only need six suitcases."

"What do you mean?"

"Three for your summer clothes and three for your winter clothes; you can always come home. Just come home."

"Well, I'll be embarrassed because this is one more failed relationship."

"It doesn't matter; you can come home."

When he said that, I immediately felt relief, like all the pressure and stress were beginning to dissipate. *It was going to be okay, and I could go home.* I hadn't stayed because I was weak; I had stayed because I was being strong, in my head. I had made my bed and was prepared to lay in it. But hearing from my brother, who had every right to judge me yet loved me anyway, gave me and my pride permission to stop the madness. As soon as we hung up the phone, I started plotting and planning. I hired a personal trainer to work with me in the building, to get those extra inches of Caribbean chicken off my thighs. I scheduled a photographer to take headshots exactly three weeks after training began. I was making all types of preparations in anticipation of my Canadian departure, without revealing that I was not going to return.

I was excited. I had learned so much in the process of working on this magazine that I was like, *shoot, I can do this kind of stuff*. I really enjoyed it, and I excelled at it. But I knew that when I got back, I was going to return to speaking and conducting workshops because I had basically given up my career to be in Canada with him. I was making money here and there but was not really able to make real money because I was an American in Canada. The Canadian loonie was worth more than the U.S. dollar, so I wasn't getting an equivalent amount. I didn't want to tell Nathan directly that I was leaving, so I told him that I was going to Maryland for a couple of weeks. It was during the time when Barack Obama was running for his first term, about a month or two before the election, and we were all rooting for Barack in Canada.

I returned to my hometown of St. Louis after a brief visit to my aunt's in Maryland. It was amazing because everybody embraced me. But I left my CD collection that I had built while working for the L.A. radio station in Canada. I had accumulated roughly 400 CDs, including some rare, collectible sets. I left them because I wanted him to believe that I was coming back, but in the back of my mind, I had always hoped that he would mail them to me once he realized that I was not returning. Dumb me because he never returned those CDs. He probably sold them to pay the rent. Yet that was a small price to pay for my freedom and the lessons learned.

What I got from Nathan is if you have a little talent, a little charm, a convincing personality and you're a workhorse, you can get anything done. He was much older than me and had never, ever found his way in more than 60 years on the planet. *What was wrong with me?* Somehow I thought I could fix him. Terrible. I couldn't. Oh yeah, he had asked me to marry him and spoke so highly of the diamond. Even going so far as to ask me if I would mind wearing a spectacular "blood diamond."

At the time, I was off my own mark and said, "No, I won't mind," enthralled in the thought that upon my next tour to Canada, I would have a big ole, glittery rock on my hand from my Caribbean man with the melodious accent. I never saw the diamond, the ring or any evidence it ever existed. And shame on me for even considering going against my morals or beliefs … accepting and wearing a blood diamond is not something to which I could truly be comfortable with. But I had been caught up. Terrible.

Dark Spaces

As a woman in my 40s, I now see life quite differently. I was optimistic, bold, fearless and a risk taker because I wouldn't take crap from anyone. Then I got soft and lowered my standards. Life happened, and certain urges filled the emotional holes left by poor choices and lack of good judgment. Getting caught up became something I learned to do. I went through a lot between college and Nathan, before the devastating blows of my future relationship with my writing partner and my second husband.

I almost lost it after Nathan. I met Jack, the retired firefighter, in St. Louis after returning to the States and just before purchasing my own home, a two-family flat brick foreclosure. It had foreclosed for nearly $150,000; I bought it for $18,000 cash. We dated and got engaged in just under a year. I was clueless as to what was really happening with him. When your partner has a disorder, or is out of order, trust me, it rubs off, and boy, did I get burned!

At 38, I was ready to be settled and at least try to pop out a kid or two, just to feel like I was contributing something good to this world. He was handsome, had great charisma, cared about serving people and came from a good, solid family. On the surface, he seemed like a great catch. We got along well, and we liked each. For a time, we really enjoyed life together. Then I started to notice a few things that were "off." In the end, though I didn't know it at the time, he was a hoarder and suffered from OCD—I think from the trauma of PTSD from his career or perhaps even from his early life, I'm really not sure. At that point, in 2008, we didn't have the reality television shows about hoarding and disorders like we do today, so I was clueless about the contradiction he was living.

The Used Flash Cubes

During the Jack days, I found I had a great aptitude for construction work. I helped him rehab a rental property and get it back on the market. Yes! Another project! When I say rehab, I was climbing up ladders, painting outside windows on the second floor, caulking, installing, building, fixing and removing the clutter. What I didn't know, I learned. With what I couldn't do, I enlisted assistance. One day, I found a brown lunch bag full of used flash cube camera bulbs, the kind we used with Kodak instant cameras back in the day when I was really young. These flashbulbs, which had four sides (a cube), are used once and then thrown away because they are one-time use bulbs. That bag had at least 20 used bulbs, no camera, no film, just used bulbs. He would not let me throw them away!!! He said he might need them for something. I did not understand. They don't make those cameras anymore. What could anyone do with those things? Nothing, absolutely nothing. So, after he left the basement, I threw them away and didn't think much more about it, other than he was strange. I was completely unaware of the damage holding onto objects and worn-out circumstances could do to the mind and body. I continued digging in. I stayed with him because that's what I thought loyalty and love were about.

He was always late. His sisters would tell him to meet them an hour before he really needed to be there so he would be on time. And when his oldest sister found out he proposed to me, under the St. Louis Gateway Arch on Christmas Day, she had a look of despair prior to her congratulatory hug. He was 14 years older than me, and he was her younger brother. She knew all about his habits and issues but really, really liked me and so did his dad, who was 91 at the time. She was happy for him and frightened for me, but didn't feel comfortable warning me about the deep-seated issues affecting her brother. She did, however, start giving me tips on how to deal with him, like telling him an earlier time to be on time.

We were engaged for eight months, without a wedding date. I wasn't comfortable setting one and avoided the topic when it came up. He didn't prefer me to travel, so I took a diversity training position at the corporate headquarters of a food-related company to get off the road, appease him and to pay for my house, which I had to rehab. That wasn't a problem since I had been a nomad for the past few years and yearned to plant roots. I had savings, a decent salary and the flexibility to continue consulting while stockpiling money for the two kitchens, two bathrooms, joists (the costly steel to support the building structure), drywall and everything else in my two-family flat. He liked me being near him, and I was settling into a comfortable little life at his house until my house was complete, right?

Once he proposed, *did I really need my house?* He had a huge one … but I had to finish my house. Since I was working full-time, he took the lead in being a junior project manager, directing workers to rip out the drop ceilings throughout the second floor. That bright idea cost me at least $5,000 because the entire place had to be dry walled, mudded and painted, which was not part of the plan that I had written down in spreadsheet form and had given to him. Whew. At the time, I didn't understand how those little things were piling up. I got it when the trash literally piled up.

Over the winter, I bundled the trash and asked him to take it out. The trash dumpster was located in the alley behind the house, which required going through the sun porch and the locked, chain-link gate. I didn't mind shared domestic duties, but I wasn't taking the trash outside; I trusted him to do it. As spring arrived and there was an early-in-the-season 55-degree day, after a bone-chilling winter, I decided to venture out to take the trash myself.

I opened the door leading to the back porch and there sat at least 20 big, black garbage bags piled up and thawing—all of the trash he supposedly took out over the winter!!! When I say I was shocked, appalled and confused at the same time, that's an understatement. When he got home, I ripped into him, and all he could say was that he needed to go through the bags to make sure there wasn't anything in there that could identify him or that didn't need to be saved. I assured him I had removed all magazine labels and blacked out any prescription bottles. It wasn't enough. The more he tried to rationalize the irrational, the more irate I became. Now the tremendous piles of *stuff* in the basement made sense. He couldn't throw anything away. I forced him to open that gate, and I marched right along with my man to that alleyway trash can, putting every single black bag in the dumpster.

Afterward, I cried. I cried for me. I cried for us. And mostly, I cried for him. In that moment, it was clear to me: he had *real problems*. Because of my ingrained habit of taking care of grown people and codependency-encouraging habits, I wouldn't leave him—he needed me. But I wanted to. I was committed to our situation but not that far gone. I knew I would never set a wedding date. Why I was willing to take one for the team and continue to deal with him has to do with my holes. It wasn't healthy or right, but it was true.

In Distress, Circa 2008

When a person is lost or operates in a dysfunctional manner, it rubs off. Yet no person, related or not, attached or not, in charge or not, is worth your sanity. During my relationship with Jack, many days I felt like I was losing my mind. I had reclaimed my life from Canada. When I met him, I hadn't been out "looking for a man." I had felt content, confident and free. I was ready to be of service again.

With Jack, suffering more than I ever had, I kept what happened in the house to myself. I was living in a fantasy land. Being tied to the wrong partner made me guilty by association. I was overwhelmed. Missing deadlines and appointments strained my business endeavors, and I behaved like a terrible friend because nobody could count on me. I couldn't count on myself. I felt immobilized. Nearly hopeless, I turned within.

I wrote this journal entry on one of those difficult days when I knew my strength alone was not enough. It's a creative writing piece written in the middle of desperation. Can you relate?

I've somehow always known that I had a message … getting to it has been tough.

It has taken me until this very moment to realize how important my message is—how important my role is—not because of title, not because of accomplishment, not because of anything I have or have not created.

My pursuit for Truth, Teaching, Learning and Service has cost me dearly.

I can't stop.

There are a few people on this earth who I love more than words, pictures, riches or gold. My goals have been to not only enjoy them, but have them enjoy me as well. Lately, I have found myself singularly focused on spreading "Absolute Good News" and have found it extremely difficult to balance home, family, career, finances and health with my own relationships; right now I am finding it difficult to balance my personal needs with those around me …

I can't stop.

Once upon a time, I was bright, I was bold, and I felt unstoppable—because I didn't know any better. People could always count on me.

Exhausted.

Today, I am doing my best to be encouraged, and I am working on my vitality, peace of mind and fixing my poor results. Most of those closest to me don't really understand because I have continued to let them down.

Please stop.

There is not enough of me to go around, and I have overcommitted myself. It used to be all about me, *not intentionally*, but in actuality.

Right now, today, in this moment, it is *intentionally* all about me—because if I don't learn how to stop, balance and incorporate the people who are most important to me, I will lose them, and I will continue to lose myself …

Can I stop?

In my classes, I have found who I am—the role I am to play in this universe. I am a communication and leadership facilitator, not because I've known so much, but because I have faltered so much. You, Lord, always work it out.

Keep going.

Kahlil Gibran once said, "Your friends are your needs answered." And sometimes my friends have been "needed" so much by me that they fled because I didn't "get" that the value was not in what we were doing, how we were doing or how fast we were doing it. It was about being together, sharing, listening, caring and, at times, just sitting, laughing and chatting. In my friends, I am able to see reflections of myself. I love them, yet sometimes I don't like what I see. I don't like what I see …

Please stay.

In my role as adult, niece, sister, fiancé and daughter, I am learning that I hurt people when I overschedule, underdeliver or am too tapped to share, listen, give or even care … I love them so much, and I am learning that I am a work in progress.

Keep living.

During my adult life, I have been a wanderer … helping others while being disconnected from those I love the most.

Today, right now, I know my value, I know my responsibility, and I also know that I have no idea how to balance all of them with all of me.

It's not over.

My prayer to my Father when in distress this morning:

In this moment, before I am late for another appointment, Father God, please help me—and please ease each of their hearts and minds—fill them up so much that somehow their anger, disappointment, pain and desire for good for me and for themselves fills them so that we can and will work through this. All of this. I can't stop.

Of myself, I can do nothing. Less of me and more of thee. Less of me and more of thee. I love you, Lord God, My Father. You know all, and I ask you to show me how to be.

In Jesus' name, thanks God, thanks God, thank you God!

Your daughter,
Jo Lena Johnson

This journal entry has been left intact.

One evening, my good girlfriend Jessica sat me down out of concern and shook me out of the fog. We discussed how I had been obsessing, trying to be productive despite the strain and pressure of being with Jack. I struggled to be free of the self-imposed hostile takeover in the hoarder's house. Given my family history of depression, I couldn't risk my life, future or work. Something had to give—and in this case, it was me. I had to give up control of a foul situation and change it. It's possible to love a person so much that you leave them because *you* have to matter first—in a self-love type of way, not in a selfish way.

Jessica was kind, loving, firm and honest about how much I had changed while involved with Jack. It's like she sensed my inner struggles and came to remind me I could fly, if I was willing to refocus and reclaim my own essence.

She used my own questions on me: *What's happening? Why is it happening? Do you want it?*

Jessica was a godsend that day, as many of my friends have been over the years. I knew the answers. I was kind of ready to go but not quite.

There were daily little mess-ups, little fibs, little mistakes, and then, one day, the water was off.

Child, when I say the water was off, it was *off*. I called him, to which he replied, "I just paid the bill; they will be there tomorrow to turn it back on."

"What??? You didn't pay the bill? It takes notice after notice before water gets turned off. What happened?"

I couldn't trust him.

At that point, I used my own questions on myself!

What's happening? Why is it happening? Do I want this? Do I deserve it? What does he need and want? What is he bringing to the table? Is there a real future here? What can we do to change things? Are we willing to change things? Are we capable of changing things? What is the healthiest choice I am willing to make today, to save my life?

Damn, Jack! Damn, Jo Lena!

He confessed that he had run out of money, was embarrassed to tell me and had tried to handle it himself. I had gone to the office supply store that day, purchasing pens, paper and other knickknacks, for which I had budgeted. It would have been no problem to give him the money, but what I didn't know did hurt me. Let's just say, he had made some bad choices during his divorce at least 10 years before, which had affected his pension because he was trying to get through the divorce instead of thinking through the matter and solving the problems. The choices caught up with him, and a portion of his retirement was being garnished, leaving him with $400 less per month than he had expected. I tried to help him straighten it out, but he wasn't even forthcoming with all that had happened. Between purchasing and rehabbing my two-family flat, rehabbing his rental property and getting caught up on his three mortgages, my savings were totally depleted, just like his.

Yep. I had made over $20,000 in the month of November 2008. So when I say by April 2009, when my house was finally done, we had two houses, were engaged and I was flat, flat broke, I mean it. Well, thanks to the job I had, I applied to get a home loan refinance, since I had already fixed the whole house. Welp, the real estate bust was upon us, and a big ole bank, who had given me a signature line of credit (out of the California banking unit, where I had opened my accounts) for $55,000, would not give me $80,000 for my house, which THEY appraised for $120,000! Well, the real estate branch of B of USA was out of the St. Louis office, and my house was located literally one block from the "good part" of St. Louis City, so I was considered to be living in the red-lined North side. I was livid. I had a high credit score, had not missed one loan payment, was current on all of my bills, but needed money for May to cover what I had spent, charged and for the monthly maintenance. Jack was unable to help, and my finances began to spiral as I believe they discriminatorily denied me. So many citizens were affected by the real estate crisis.

In the meantime, I had become disenchanted at my corporate position. They didn't really want diversity; they wanted the classes, but not the reality of fixing *broken conditions*. I ended up losing my voice, literally, and was out on disability because the doctors at one of the best university hospitals in St. Louis could not figure out what was wrong with me. Me, Jo Lena Johnson, world-renowned trainer, speaker, coach, could not speak!!! I was getting 80% of my salary, so I was bringing in over $5,000 a month when I applied for the loan. But by that time, I had let go of my other clients; I had too much on my plate. However, six days before the loan was denied, I went back to work and was let go. I cannot discuss what happened legally, but justice was served in the long run—it just took a while to get my settlement. Since I technically had no job when I was denied the loan, I couldn't start the process all over again at another bank without real employment.

I don't even know how I made it. I told you, I was losing it. I still had my own house, thank goodness.

Getting a tenant in the lower apartment was supposed to give me relief. However, I thought going through Section 8 would give me guaranteed rent and a good experience. The rent came; the experience wasn't a good one, though. It wasn't until September when my tenant was able to move in. Jack and I still had not set a wedding date—I had big doubts but was remaining loyal. I still had my upstairs apartment, the one I had planned to live in when I purchased the property. Since money was tight and I was at Jack's, I rented my unit. Less than six weeks later, following another series of little challenges, he told me he didn't want to get married and wanted to break up. He did what I should have done, and probably would have done, had my house been free and my bank account been right. We were way too different, and neither of us were really going to change. I was tired of the issues and wanted to be free, but I didn't have the courage to stop the madness. I was depleted.

"Really Jack??? I just rented both of my units and now you tell me you want to break up? Well, I'm not going anywhere because I have nowhere to go and I'm not renting from someone else." I felt well within my rights to live there on his dime at that point. I had poured so much sweat equity into his properties and actual cash into the household. He owed me, and both of us knew it.

At that point, breaking up was absolutely best for both of us. However, I wasn't going to incur more expense because he spoke up. He was paying every bill in that house by that point, so I let him pay. I needed a reprieve. I moved into the second-floor, two-room suite of his home. We were practicing abstinence and had only been intimate a few times. Things worked well, there was sexual compatibility, but we were trying to do things the right way, even though we were living together. So moving to the other bedroom was no big deal; we weren't doing anything anyway. He moved upstairs to the attic after he allowed his master bedroom to become totally and completely run over by his clothes and other old things. You couldn't even see the bed. Since he was no longer trying to impress me or hide his tendencies, he showed it all. Thank goodness he was a "clean" hoarder. His finances were in great shape thanks to my contributions and strategies, but my credit sank as I couldn't keep up with the new bills. Deeper holes.

Then Jack, the retired firefighter, my former fiancé, started dating, while I was living there. That hurt. I wasn't into him like that anymore; however, the thought that he would blatantly start seeing someone so quickly after we officially ended was something I never considered he would do. I think he met her while we were officially a couple, as she went to his church and became interested in him. I was stuck until one of my tenants moved out. It was a long, long few months, trapped in the hoard and coming to grips with what my life had become. Feeling as if I was burned to a crisp, I learned a lot about life, about love and about myself.

New Places

I realized I didn't know what love was—healthy love. Independent yet cohesive love. Honest yet human love. Responsible yet patient love. Unattached yet connected love. Passionate and peaceful love. I had learned bad habits along my way. And without children, I didn't really feel needed or appreciated, let alone loved, cherished and adored, which I truly wanted. I was broken, and there was only one man to fix me. I recommitted to reading the Bible several times a day just to have clarity, peace of mind and to make it through my pain and sorrow. I was sorry for so much. Not just God and me, but for all the holes along the way. It had been over 15 years since I studied to become a teacher (the first step to ministry) back in Los Angeles, at Della Reese's church, Understanding Principles for Better Living. I knew what I had to do: prayer in action. I started studying again. I started finding joy, delight and wisdom in the Psalms, Proverbs and especially in the stories of Ruth and Esther. I absolutely dived in and began the process of reclaiming my birthright—being a child of the Living God. I also started attending different churches to see where I fit in St. Louis. Everything was so much different than in L.A. and D.C. I questioned everything about myself, my sanity, my pitiful little heart and my stupid choices. I was able to see that I couldn't do anything on my own. I had nothing left. That actually turned out to be a good place because I gave God my brokenness and started trusting Him with everything. I sought counseling, in addition to my Bible work and my church work, and finished writing the three books I had started writing simultaneously.

Right around this time, my precious niece was born and then my precious aunt passed in D.C. I gained an angel and lost an angel. It was sooooo tough. I lived in that suite and did my best to gain what I had lost in terms of my spirit, my mind, my body and my soul. Through months of rigorous working, planning and serving, I stayed steadfast. After several delays, my upstairs tenant finally moved out. I had the carpet cleaned 30 minutes after she left, and the next day moved all of my things into the apartment with the help of my stepdad. We were tired, worn out actually, after all the trips. But he was kind, oh so kind, to help me, his poor child finding her way again. He's never judged me. He's just loved me through it all, offering sound wisdom and advice and his shoulder to cry on during my various calamities.

Once in my apartment, I realized that my downstairs tenant was irresponsible and trifling. She moved out with her two little boys, and I got a new tenant, a single woman, a little older than me. I kept studying, started doing more work, especially in writing and publishing, and began coaching others through the process, learning through my own mistakes and victories. I was on a good track. I began to be healthy again, my finances increased, my mind was clear, my heart was mending, and my energy was back. I was reading, praying and healing. I went to church, and I also had a real relationship with God, my Father. I felt safe. I was becoming whole. Months went by; I had some suitors. I casually dated but nothing worth noting. I was just joyful. I did some book launches around the country, picked up more authors and was flourishing again. I was in such a good space and grateful for my past and what I had been through.

And then I met the Chief.

Peeling Through the Pain

Late in the midnight hour, when wrenching in pain, I learned, instead of leaning on myself or somebody else, to go to a higher place when I'm at my lowest. Many nights I was by myself, and even when I wasn't, humans don't meet our expectations, let alone those of others. Relying on someone else, who has their own issues, to fix you doesn't work. I may get sad or weepy, but I don't give up because I cannot give up. When I wanted to roll in a ball and die, I would cry. Those tears started transforming me from holding in the pain to letting it out. In bursts, over time, the pain would ooze out, peeling. Life's layers are like onions—they can sting, they can stink, yet they are flavorful and lend robustness to the recipe when prepared the right way. Peeling works.

If you've been on the planet long enough to remember the "I Love Lucy" television show, think about all those times she managed to get into trouble, and by the end of the episode, all was well after a great adventure. That's how blessed I have been! Sure, I get into trouble. Sometimes I'm my own worst enemy. And sometimes, I'm just minding my own *clean colored business* when things happen. No matter what, no matter how disappointed or troubled I seemed to be, I made it through. I've had a lot of amazing experiences and unique victories. This has been a little glimpse into my life. I continue to stand, but not by myself.

I am sharing this poem with you because at a very, very deep level, this is my life. I embrace it and I am grateful through it all. Getting through it all is the key—not holding on, or staying in it, but peeling through what's no longer needed to get down to the juice, the flavor and your goodness. May you find your methods and answers, peeling.

> In you, Lord, I have taken refuge;
> let me never be put to shame.
> In your righteousness, rescue me and deliver me;
> turn your ear to me and save me.
> Be my rock of refuge,
> to which I can always go;
> give the command to save me,
> for you are my rock and my fortress.
> Deliver me, my God, from the hand of the wicked,
> from the grasp of those who are evil and cruel.
>
> For you have been my hope, Sovereign Lord,
> my confidence since my youth.
> From birth I have relied on you;

you brought me forth from my mother's womb.
I will ever praise you.
I have become a sign to many;
you are my strong refuge.
My mouth is filled with your praise,
declaring your splendor all day long.

Do not cast me away when I am old;
do not forsake me when my strength is gone.
For my enemies speak against me;
those who wait to kill me conspire together.
They say, "God has forsaken him;
pursue him and seize him,
for no one will rescue him."
Do not be far from me, my God;
come quickly, God, to help me.
May my accusers perish in shame;
may those who want to harm me
be covered with scorn and disgrace.

As for me, I will always have hope;
I will praise you more and more.

My mouth will tell of your righteous deeds,
of your saving acts all day long—
though I know not how to relate them all.
I will come and proclaim your mighty
acts, Sovereign Lord;
I will proclaim your righteous deeds, yours alone.
Since my youth, God, you have taught me,

and to this day I declare your marvelous deeds.
Even when I am old and gray,
do not forsake me, my God,
till I declare your power to the next generation,
your mighty acts to all who are to come.

Your righteousness, God, reaches to the heavens,
you who have done great things.
Who is like you, God?
Though you have made me see troubles,
many and bitter,
you will restore my life again;
from the depths of the earth
you will again bring me up.
You will increase my honor
and comfort me once more.

I will praise you with the harp
for your faithfulness, my God;
I will sing praise to you with the lyre,
Holy One of Israel.
My lips will shout for joy
when I sing praise to you—
I whom you have delivered.
My tongue will tell of your righteous acts
all day long,
for those who wanted to harm me
have been put to shame and confusion.

Psalm 71 (NIV)

Epilogue

"Patience is bitter, but its fruit is sweet." – Aristotle

Acknowledging My Mom's Position

I went to my mom's house to read this book to her. Because I was sharing personal stories from her life that had affected mine, it was her right to at least know what I had said. I was nervous and afraid—not about the content, but how she would take it. I'm pleased to say that we were together for seven hours that Wednesday evening in October. Through tears, bits of anger and many "oh really" moments, we made it through—without outside intervention!

During the first chapters, Mom began giving me her insights about things that had occurred. Because I was young, there were certain things I didn't know. She explained more about how she had felt during her marriages, why she felt it was important to get divorced and also discussed her challenges with depression, along with being hospitalized as a result. She really surprised me. When we got to the portion of the book when I said, "I think it was the white guy who took her over the edge," she told me it wasn't him—that he was nice to her and that she still respected him. But that it had been the loss of her father years before that had changed her, seemingly, forever.

"It wasn't him; I had not gotten over my father's death," she said.

I was a freshman in high school when we got the call that my grandpa had been killed in a tragic accident. He worked in a place that had something to do with trains, where the huge train doors hung from cranes. One of the cranes gave way, and the train door crushed him. Though I knew she missed him tremendously, I believe all of us underestimated the impact of his death on her. She admitted that losing her dad caused her to question her faith, God and life itself. She said, "I didn't want to live anymore. I was angry at God. I lost my faith. I didn't want to live." I was sad to hear her pain and hurt regarding grandpa, and God. Holes, holes and more holes. For many years, the passing of her father has continued to contribute to her *Broken Conditions*.

The Trumpet Player Was Talented and Unique

It wasn't just dazzle that had her intrigued with the Trumpet Player. It was the feeling of a connection to a bigger world that was compelling and previously unknown to her. After I heard her describe him—the person between the two big encounters I had had with him—whom she loved, I understood and related.

"Harrison could play almost any instrument, and he could play just about any tune by hearing it one time. He started touring professionally when he was 14 years old, during the summers. I liked his personality. He was fun, and I so enjoyed how we danced together. He was also so intelligent, smart and worldly. He had been a paratrooper. He had lived an interesting life. He was knowledgeable and educated and had a lot of insight into things I was not privy to. That night when we met him, he was playing Oliver Sain's music. Oliver was a St. Louis local and that song, 'Soul Serenade,' was nine minutes or so long. Whenever I saw him, I would say, 'Oliver, play my song for me,' and he would. So when I saw Harrison playing that song, I loved it."

"Interesting," with a smile on my face, I replied.

And, "No, I would not have taken them home if you were not with me. I felt more comfortable driving them because you were there."

She added, "Yes, he had a convertible; it was a Triumph with a black top in olive green. It was at a repair shop where they only worked on foreign cars. It never seemed to run right after each shop visit, so after a while, it was going to be so expensive, he let it go. That's when he ended up getting the truck."

She also clarified about why the Trumpet Player was angry and broke into the house. She had broken up with him because she didn't see a future with him. He was angry and didn't want to let go. She stood firm, knowing she needed to move on from that relationship. He was unwilling.

I realized that, unknowingly, I had done the same thing she had—fallen for men because of their qualities and then found it hard to escape … this is ugly and beautiful … yet part of the healing I had with my mother.

When I left her house that evening, we kissed and hugged, both emotionally spent as a result of our time together. The next day, I stopped by her place briefly after a long and taxing meeting. I was hungry, tired and wanted to climb into my bed … 30 minutes away. When she said, "Jo, I wanted to say something about yesterday," I immediately cringed and braced myself for whatever puncture may be delivered. And do you know what?

She said, "It's not bad. I just want to thank you for reading the story to me. I guess you should have interviewed me before because you would have understood and so would I, a lot sooner. I am glad we did that, and I think it will bring us closer." Though she did not want me to talk about "her personal business," she got that what happened in our lives is intertwined, for better or worse.

God had answered my prayers from the night before with

a fairly easy exchange and then this! My mother and I had gained insight, perspective, mutual understanding and respect as a result of sharing what was written and then discussing how the events affected her life and my life. Several layers of hurt felt as if they were peeling off and we were closer to the core of our true selves—and our deep love for one another.

Mom heard me because, since it was written, I felt safe in "saying it." And I learned so much about her, her choices and how much influence her parents had on her—when she was growing up, and even at nearly 70 years old. Generations are affected by our choices, and that was evident through our dialogue.

From my heart, I can only hope and pray that you, too, receive a blessing from spending time with *Broken Conditions* and the other books in the series. I am a believer; however, I don't impose what I believe, and I simply share from my perspective—the good and the bad times. I do believe the things I discuss in these books, my experiences (personally and professionally) and my willingness to pour out my soul to others are part of my purpose on earth, and much bigger than me. It is my belief that God orchestrated an awesome and unique opportunity for us as mother and daughter to connect, and I encourage you to do the same ... connect with those entangled in your *Broken Conditions* so that you can release them, you and the situations, to move forward. I am grateful and wanted you to know how much I appreciate my Mom for giving us the space. It is my hope and faith that serve as my encouragement as we each move from here.

"Jesus turned and saw her. 'Take heart, daughter,' he said, 'your faith has healed you.' And the woman was healed at that moment." – Matthew 9:22 (NIV)

Excerpt from

THE CLEAN COLORED GIRL CHRONICLES
VOLUME 2:

Back to Friday, August 27th

Kim was at the Black Expo party. She walked over; we exchanged greetings, and she said, "Let me introduce you to my friend."

I left my table and walked over to her table.

She said, "Sebastian, this is Jo Lena; Jo Lena, this is Sebastian."

I immediately recognized him as someone who I had gone to high school with, although I had never known his name. I remember he was wearing a black velvet jacket. He attended the party with his boss and coworker, who he introduced me to. He was smooth. As the loud music played, he leaned in close, listening to every word I said. When he spoke, he had my attention. That's how I found out he was a chief in the Navy and was going to be sponsoring a diversity event with NSBE, the National Society of Black Engineers. I was excited to meet a fellow Gardens graduate who was succeeding in his career. And the NSBE event would be a great place for me to speak. While we were listening and sharing, I slipped in a little hint about putting me in contact with someone from the organization.

LaToya indicated that she was ready to go, but I was having such a good time with Sebastian, I wasn't ready to leave and got a little upset that she was.

I asked LaToya to hold on for a minute, turned back to Sebastian and asked, "Are you dating Kim?"

He emphatically said, "NO."

I was a bit surprised by the passion in his no and was delighted by the answer itself, which meant we would surely continue our conversation. I gave him my business card and said goodbye.

On our way out the door, Kim came over, put her arm in my arm and said, "Yes girl, me and Sebastian have been through evvveryyything together."

When she said *"everything,"* it clicked that less than two months before, the man girdle guy had mentioned Kim's knack for blocking. So, I took her comment as a sign that

that's what she was trying to do again. *She couldn't be dating Sebastian, right?* I saw her with that man, and the month in between when we were speaking about a potential business transaction, she was talking about a man (I assumed that same man) whom she needed to let go. However, that guy was not Sebastian. I took Sebastian for his word and placed Kim in the file cabinet of my mind marked "Blocker." Not upset, just believing she wanted all the men for herself.

When LaToya and I finally got into the car, I said, "Girl, I think I really like him. He reminds me of Denzel."

Sunday

The next day, I remember wondering if Sebastian was going to call. Since he lived in Memphis, I thought it would be a nice opportunity to see each other before he left town. Nope.

When the phone rang on Sunday, sure enough, it was him.

I asked, "Are you calling for business or pleasure?"

"Well, both."

I was definitely down for that, but I was with a client and couldn't speak freely, so I told him that I would call him back. Four hours later, I returned his call and was disappointed when I had to leave a message. He called the next morning while on his way to work. We started talking daily. During one of our many conversations, I asked the question, *"What is a man like you doing single?"*

He admitted that he had been in a serious relationship with a woman he had planned to marry, but it was over and he was just waiting for her to get all of her stuff out of his house. That was pretty interesting because my former fiancé was Jack and his former fiancé's name was Jackie. A little ironic, don't you think? Jack and I broke up in October 2009; however, I continued to live with him for several months after our breakup because I had rented out my house and my rental property. I was not willing to pay for another place to live under the circumstances so I stayed in my second-floor suite at his home, recovering from our breakup. Once we broke up, we never went back. We were housemates without benefits. I moved into my house in March, healing, becoming happy again and living freely in my own space. So I did not have a problem with Sebastian's situation because I knew that it was possible to live in the same space with someone you used to be in love with and have no feelings at all.

I was naïve to think that Sebastian and Jackie were living like me and Jack, without benefits. I did not consider that at the time, but I surely should have.

Eventually a Sordid Past Comes to Light

Later on, when talking with friends about Sebastian, I remembered that he was the guy two girls had been fighting about in the classroom during his senior year. Yes, they had a physical altercation in class over that young man. Soon, one of his former football teammates found out that we were dating and immediately called me.

He then proceeded to tell me stories about a mutual associate with whom Sebastian had been having relations (Kim). To which I responded, "Oh, I know about her. He's okay."

"Well, I just wanted to warn you," skeptically, as he said goodbye. That guy was a good friend who didn't have to call me, and boy, do I wish I had listened to his advice …

Connect with Jo Lena and the Clean Colored Girl Movement

Order: Lady and the Chief, Volume 2

Order: Married and Divorced in the Same Year, Volume 3

JoLenaJohnson.com

Discussion Book Club Questions

1. How did you feel reading the book? Sad, empathetic, angry?

2. Could you relate to the circumstances or choices the author made in the book?

3. What did you learn about Jo Lena after reading this book?

4. Were you able to relate to her story? How was it or was it not relatable?

5. What did you think about her relationship with her mother? How would you have handled it?

6. How did her mother's choices influence her relationships?

7. How would you have handled the Trumpet Player?

8. How important is the mother/daughter relationship regarding relationships with a significant other?

9. Are there any relationships mentioned in the book that you want to learn more about?

10. What do you think about Jo Lena's need to help people?

11. Can you relate to the Peeling Through the Pain chapter? Did it make a difference once you noticed the origin of the text?

12. What did you like/not like about the book?

@ Jo Lena Johnson, The AG Resilience Coach

@JoLenaJohnson

@JoLena Johnson

@JoLenaJohnson

Website: JoLenaJohnson.com

Jo Lena welcomes email from readers at AuthenticJo@AbsoluteGood.com

The Clean Colored Girl Association

We stay connected internationally through a group hosted on Facebook. In person, we are forming chapters around the country. It's time for women to connect through life and struggles, coming out better, on the other side.

About the Author

Jo Lena Johnson, the woman, has a secret life. She paints houses to relax and recharge. Covered in paint, spattered with caulk, she finds it relaxing and productive, transforming one room at a time. The woman loves projects and enjoys letting the creative juices flow! Jo Lena Johnson, the AG Resilience Coach, is a certified mediator, international trainer, acclaimed author, and founder and CEO of Absolute Good Training and Life Skills Management. Principle-focused, results-driven and heart-centered, Jo Lena has taught nearly 100,000 people worldwide with her no-nonsense and dynamic approach, with messages of how to effectively communicate, manage conflict and maintain, even after something bad happens (resilience). Become uniquely self-aware, unburdened, enlightened and empowered through spending time with Jo Lena. For personal, professional or group coaching, consultation, mediation, conflict management, workshops, author/book development services or to hire Jo Lena as a keynote speaker, reach out today.

www.ingramcontent.com/pod-product-compliance
Lightning Source LLC
Chambersburg PA
CBHW052027290426
44112CB00014B/2404